SHARING A Fly Wing

A Memoir of Growing Up on Virgin Gorda, British Virgin Islands

HILDEGARDE FLAX-SHAW

This book is a work of non-fiction. Names, places and incidents are the product of the author's childhood memories and simply meant to memorialize a time long past. Any resemblance to persons other than the ones listed here are purely coincidental. At the time of printing my siblings were aware of their inclusion and no objections were voiced.

Copyright © 2021 by Hildegarde Flax-Shaw
Case Number: 1-10860147771

ISBN: Hardcover 978-1-7363259-0-2
      Softcover 978-1-7363259-1-9

All rights reserved. No part of this publication may be reproduced, distributed, or transmitted in any form or by any means, including photocopying, recording, or other electronic or mechanical methods, without the prior written permission from the copyright owner.

This book was printed in the United States of America.

To order additional copies of this book, please contact:

Hildegarde Flax-Shaw
772 Bonnie Claire Drive
Walnut, CA 91789
hildeshaw@gmail.com
www.hildeshaw.com

First Edition
Title Inspiration from Mother's Life Lesson

SHARING A FLY WING

A Memoir of Growing Up on Virgin Gorda, British Virgin Islands

Hildegarde Flax-Shaw

Also by this Author

A collection of short stories published on the author's professional website:

-Sometimes It Takes a Village

-Snowflakes

-A Bloody Mess

-Walking in Their Shoes

~*Dedication*~

To my children, Gayle and Dana-

You are the treasures of my life

"The beauty that surrounds me is absolutely breathtaking....
It is the faces of my children."

Anabela Lourier

~Table of Contents~

Illustrations viii

Key Words and Interpretations xii

Foreword xv

Acknowledgements xvi

Introduction 1

Prologue 6

A Rich, Colourful History 8

Protected Areas of Interest 23

Virgin Gorda as I Knew It 37

My One-Room Schoolhouse – A Dilapidated Shack 49

House of My Childhood 68

Mother – A Woman of Strength Unfailing 80

Reading – A Family Affair 102

Gastronomic Delights 111

Superstitions, Ghosts and Jumbies... 122

Christmases Past 128

Playing House 142

My Tata – A Privileged Man 146

Declining Customs... 162

Mamina – Our Loving Family Matriarch 169

Special Memories of My Siblings and Me 177

Mother-isms 185

In Memoriam – My Siblings Lost... 189

A Letter to My Beloved Parents... 195

Epilogue 200

Accolades for the Author 204

Bibliography 208

About the Author... 210

~Illustrations~

Unless otherwise noted, all photographs are the personal property of the author. Written permission was obtained for all others.

Goats in the Road..10

Nail Bay Sugar Works..12

Map of Virgin Gorda..15

Road to the Baths...17

Iguana on Long Road...19

Coastline at Copper Mine Point......................................21

Sea Grapes 22

The Baths 24

The Baths 27

Pitch Apple Tree...28

Devil's Bay	30
Rock Formation at Spring Bay/The Crawl	32
Spring Bay/The Crawl	33
Ruins of the Coppermine	35
Uncle Bregado	39
The Fowl Cock	43
St. Mary's School	50
Aesop's Fables	55
Source: Children's Encyclopedia	57
The House of My Childhood	69
Traditional Coal-pot	73
Badin' Pan and Scrub Board	76
The Clothes Iron or Goose	77
Mother and Tata	81
Mother Making a Placemat	89
Brick Oven	92
Aunt Conce	98
Uncle Tom's Cabin	103
My Holy Bible	106
On Her Wedding Morn'	107

Grafted Mango 112

Humming Top 133

Doll's Tea Set 134

Jacks 135

Flycatchers 139

Cousin Yvonne and Nennie 141

Oona and Goldilocks 143

Yellow Love Plant 144

Tata as a Young Man 147

The Flax Building 150

Tata with the Boys' Brigade 154

Tata's Lion Club Plaque 155

Soursop 157

Sugar apple 158

Uncle Hartman 159

Tata as Foreman – clearing road to Little Dix Bay 161

Cashew Tree /cherry tree 163

Genips 165

Coal-pit 166

Mamina 170

Aloe Vera 174

Mamina's Letter to Me 176

Me 181–183

My Dear, Dear Mother 188

"You have brains in your head,
You have feet in your shoes
You can steer yourself in any direction you choose.
You are off to great places
Today is your day
Your mountain is waiting
So get on your way."

Dr. Seuss

~Key Words and Interpretations~

Ah come	I come
Badin pan	washpan
Bawbaw	new baby
Belonger	Virgin Islander
Carto	cardboard
Chamber pot	pan used for urination at night
Cotta	cloth put on the head for carrying a load
Curuttle	junk, useless items
De	the
'Foreday	before day, early morning
Fowl cock	rooster
Frock	dress
Grinning	laughing
Ah gone	goodbye, I am leaving
In the way	pregnant

Jags	slits on meat or fish to hold seasoning
Johnny cake	fried bread
Jumbie	ghost or evil spirit
Lemme	let me, allow me
Licks	lashes from the headmaster's belt
Local constable	policeman without a firearm
Long meter	a person who likes to talk
Melee` or strumoo	gossip or scandal
Ole Year's Night	New Year's Eve
Ole time	long ago
Oryuh	you and yours
Pantaloon	pants
Pate`	fried, meat-filled turnover /pastry
Pear	avocado
Plats	braids
Poachie	pan used for urination at night
Provisions	sweet potatoes, cassava, tannia
Pudging	diarrhea
Registrar	recorder of births and deaths
Rigmarole	confusion, gossip
Rounders	baseball
Spittle	saliva

Standards	grades
Stick	constable's baton
Taunts/Taunie	another name for "Aunt"
The Rock	Virgin Gorda
Tommon	Tamarind
Trunk	wooden box used for luggage or storage
Burden	the unborn baby

~Foreword~

Hilde has woven her childhood and teenage memories into a cultural tapestry illustrating the traditions and customs of her home island, Virgin Gorda and the British Virgin Islands, in the 1950s.

As she pays tribute to her parents, teachers and ancestors, the real culture bearers, the character and values of community life are also highlighted. We learn of the island's cuisine, its people, ole time sayings and meanings and the glue that holds a community together.

The book preserves some aspects of Virgin Islands' cultural heritage for generations yet unborn. It should make additional reading material in the islands' schools.

Verna Penn Moll
November 12, 2019

~Acknowledgements~

> *"If you wish your merit to be known, acknowledge that of other people."*
>
> Proverb

I often secretly wished that my children could have experienced life as I knew it in the 1950's and early 60's growing up on Virgin Gorda. I sometimes shared tidbits of that life with them and they were always amazed that I could have survived a life without telephones and television. As the years went by, I always thought that someday I would make notes for them about this life they found so interesting. However, it was my many conversations with my friend, Kelly while we awaited the arrival of our patients at work that was the impetus behind actually getting started with this book. She said that my life had been a fascinating one and encouraged me to memorialize it in a book. Kelly, as you can see, I took your advice to heart and my children are grateful.

My deepest gratitude goes to my brother Ellsworth, known to all as Boy Blue, and his wife Andria, herself an accomplished author, who encouraged me to get on with the writing of this book, and who frequently inquired about its progress.

A special thank you goes to Lisa, my son's fiancée who assisted me with the final processes of editing and formatting before going to print. You were all the "wind beneath my wings."

I would be remiss if I did not acknowledge my Elementary School teacher, Mr. Alfred Christopher, who inspired my great love of writing. His essay assignments based on quirky topics opened the floodgates of my creative thinking and writing and encouraged me to put pen to paper. I will be forever indebted to him.

It is with a deep sense of gratitude and honour that I acknowledge my beloved parents, Mother and Tata. They were themselves avid readers who inspired my love of reading at an early age by filling our home with books of various authors and subjects… of fiction, and non-fiction, of poetry and Greek mythology, and the Holy Bible which they reverently referred to as the "Good Book."

I feel blessed that in later years when I presented some of my research papers to my nursing professors a few of them wrote suggestive comments - " *you should write for publication*" - in the margins. I just knew that I loved writing, but I thank God that they also gave me food for thought.

Lastly, I acknowledge you my dear readers. Thank you for taking the time to share the memories I hold dear….. the memories that evoke nostalgia when I least expect it. I hope that by strolling down my memory lane with me, you will be inspired to visit Virgin Gorda, to meet our people, to explore our island with its magnificent beaches, sample our cuisine and learn about some of the customs that make us a unique people, because no life would be complete without exploring one of "Nature's little Secrets."

> *"You don't have to be responsible for someone's feelings to acknowledge them."*
> Michael P. Nichols

~Introduction~

> *"When you want something, all the universe conspires to help you."*
>
> Paulo Coelho

The transition from "there" to "here," from "child" to "nurse" surfaced when I was about eight years old - it was all that I wanted to be when I grew up; over time *"I want to be a nurse"* became my mantra. Tata boldly voiced his objections and Mother very quietly said, *"maybe one day."* The sleepy, undeveloped island of Virgin Gorda with its one-room schoolhouse offered no opportunity in this regard, so when I became older my parents allowed me to attend school abroad so that my dream would be realized.

Saying goodbye to my Tata, my sister and brothers was not easy, but it was made a little more bearable by Mother traveling with me. I was seventeen years old. We spent two days in St. Thomas before continuing to New York. I looked forward to my arrival there with great teenage enthusiasm. I was fashionably dressed in a pale-yellow *frock* and matching high-heeled pumps, ready for the big city! On arrival, I was both happy and a little overwhelmed.... it was a gigantic place with lots of activity and more people than I had ever seen in one place; it was totally unlike the one I had known for seventeen years.

There were cars and television and movies and shops, storefronts with beautiful things for sale displayed in the windows, none of which I had ever seen. My Uncle Eddie who was Mother's brother living in New York, took us to Radio City Music Hall to see the world-famous dancers known as the Rockettes. We also saw a well-known actress, Doris Day, in a movie with lots of soap suds! I found it all very entertaining. I wondered if Virgin Gorda would ever have anything to compare. This was going to be quite an adventure!

In New York I lived with Mother's cousin, Aunt Nina and her family but I missed mine terribly. From time to time waves of nostalgia enveloped me, and I cried quietly in the safety of my room. I longed for the dirt roads and the moonlit nights of home. I missed seeing the neighbours' cows and goats meandering along the roads….and where were the beaches? I longed to go in the sea. I often reminded myself that I wanted to become a nurse and it was necessary for me to be away from my family.

I disliked the vastness of the city and of having to ride a train to get to my chosen destination - I did not like rushing at great speeds through a tunnel and being unable to see where I was going. I did not like the noise of hundreds of cars and I hated that people hurried along, minding their business and not saying "good morning" or "good afternoon" to each other as we did on Virgin Gorda.

What kind of place was this? This was New York life and I had chosen to live here so that I could become a nurse. I quickly learned that adjustment was the key to coping with the things that were different from the world I had known. This was my new home after all.

In his eighth novel, *"David Copperfield,"* Charles Dickens wrote that the character would determine whether or not he was the hero of his own life. I decided that I would be the best student I could be and make my parents proud of me. I would be the hero of my life! My parents had certainly given me a good, strong, moral upbringing and a faith which would help me to cope with any challenges I faced.

I wrote letters to my parents quite often but it was usually three or four weeks (or longer), before they completed the journey through the intricate postal system in the islands. Virgin Gorda was a place without telephones, so speaking with my family was not an option.

Over the years as I returned home for short visits, I was always dismayed to find that no significant progress had come to the island. Even so, I was always happy to go home. All of Virgin Gorda knew of my impending visit as Tata could not keep the news to himself. He always said that he would be overjoyed if all of his children lived in the Virgin Islands close to him. Toward that end, each time I went home he started his campaign to convince me to return to Virgin Gorda on a permanent basis.

Each chapter in this book represents a childhood memory which was made even more special by the purity and innocence of that time. It is my hope that by reading of Virgin Gorda's history and sharing my memories you will, in your mind's eye, be transported with me to that time and place where I spent the first seventeen years of my life.

Travel and Leisure Magazine's description is enticing: *"White sand beaches, swaying palm fronds, friendly locals and fresh fruits and drinks—is there a more peaceful, relaxing place* on Earth than the British Virgin Islands? If you're in the mood for a beach getaway, travel to Virgin Gorda, the third largest isle in the BVI, and maybe the most idyllic. With its pristine beaches, turquoise water, astonishing landscapes, and fantastic villas and restaurants, a trip to Virgin Gorda is nothing short of paradise."

I derived much pleasure from writing this book and at times I became a bit nostalgic as I recalled those wonderful days of my childhood. My wish is that while reading you will be able to envision the simplicity of our lives, the bonds of family and friendships of the island's inhabitants, the raw innocence and playfulness of our carefree children, the riches found in the traditions and beliefs we have always held dear as well as the kaleidoscope of natural beauty that is inherent in our beautiful, tropical island.

> *"In a sense, each of us is an island.*
> *In another sense, however, we are all one.*
> *For though islands appear separate, and may be situated*
> *at great distances from one another, they are only*
> *extrusions of the same planet…. Earth.*
>
> J. Donald Walters

~*Prologue*~

"Sometimes you will never know the value of a moment until it becomes a memory."

Dr. Seuss

It is my day off from work, but I automatically wake at 4:45 a.m. although I have not set the alarm. I feel a moment of temporary annoyance, but quickly realize that my body is simply attuned to my work schedule. I pull my covers up to my ears and savour the thought that I will not have to get up and go to work. My work as a Registered Nurse has been the greatest passion of my life but yesterday was another horrendously busy day in my department and I am happy to be at home today.

As I lie in bed, I become aware of the pitter-patter of raindrops outside on the pavement. I get up and look out of the window and see that the torrential rain is coming down in proverbial sheets, creating large puddles on the lawn. I see a couple of frogs jumping about in the water and I wonder where they came from. I had never seen them before.

The sky is dark and ominous looking, as if it could envelop the house at any moment. The chimes on the patio are making their own orchestral music as they are tossed about by gusts of wind and heavy rain. For once, the weather forecast is accurate. I hastily crawl back under the covers with a big grin on my face. My love of the rain is unparalleled! It evokes myriad, happy memories of growing up in the British Virgin Islands on the island of Virgin Gorda a lifetime ago.

"Memory is the treasure house of the mind
Wherein the monuments thereof are kept and preserved."

Thomas Fuller

~A Rich, Colourful History~

"Don't listen to what they say –go see."
Author unknown

I am proud to have been born a Virgin Gordian and always look forward with great anticipation to my visits there. I usually fly into St. Thomas, then take a ferry across to Tortola and another to Virgin Gorda. It is a good feeling - one of great pride - to be referred to by Immigration officials as a *"belonger"* as they scan my passport and see my birthplace.

There was always something almost magical about the ferry approaching the island, knowing that my Tata (and sometimes, Mother), would be waiting on the wharf for me......and then, savouring the thought that *"I am home."* In order to provide you, my dear readers, with a good understanding of this environment in which I grew up, and before I delve into my memories of what life was like then, I will first share with you a little of Virgin Gorda's history – and a colourful one it was!

According to the Government of the British Virgin Islands (BVI) the territory is comprised of Tortola, Virgin Gorda, Anegada, and Jost Van Dyke, along with over forty-two smaller islands and cays. Many of the islands are uninhabited and governed by Queen Elizabeth ll. Virgin Gorda is located between the deep turquoise waters of the North Atlantic Ocean and the sparkling Caribbean Sea and is part of the group known as the Lesser Antilles.

The climate is tropical and influenced by trade winds. A bright sunny day may be interrupted from time to time by short, unexpected bursts of showers, which is not unusual in tropical climates. Temperatures range from the mid 70's Fahrenheit in the early months of the year to mid 90's during the summer months. These islands are subject to hurricanes which occur anytime during the months of June through November.

Virgin Gorda was listed among the "Best Islands" in Travel and Leisure Magazine in 2012, 2013 and 2014. It continues to enjoy fame in many upscale travel magazines and its location is no longer a mystery to travelers seeking exotic places for their vacations.

It is hailed for its spectacular beaches with white, powdery sand, and if privacy and seclusion are desired, you will not be disappointed when visiting some of these beaches.

It is an idyllic destination for honeymooners and is a place where goats and cattle stroll leisurely along the roads, at times appearing to own the right of way to traffic.

Goats in the Road

The history books are teeming with the adventures of Christopher Columbus and they tell us that he discovered the Virgin Islands during his second voyage. He dubbed them Santa Ursula y las once mil Vírgenes (Saint Ursula and her 11,000 Virgins), according to the legend of St. Ursula, a Romano- British princess who was believed to have been a Christian martyr in Cologne, Germany in the year 383 C.E. This exceptionally long title was later abbreviated to "the Virgins." Columbus was reportedly the first European visitor to the island.

The profile of the island on the horizon resembled a "fat virgin" lying on her side in the water, so he named it Virgin Gorda, the Spanish translation of which is "virgin fat woman." Fat virgin or not, the travel advertisements very accurately describe it as one of "Nature's little Secrets."

Virgin Gorda boasts a colourful history of long ago being occupied by the Arawak and Carib Indians who farmed and fished the island's then abundant natural resources. Legend has it that notorious pirates like Bluebeard and Captain Kidd also occupied the island and preyed on Spanish galleons (warships later used for trade in the 15th-17th centuries) as they navigated the treacherous reefs of the Caribbean waters on a regular basis.

Virgin Gorda held an attraction not only for the Indians but the Dutch as well. In 1631, the Dutch West India Company became interested in rumours of copper on Virgin Gorda and as a result of that interest a settlement was established on Virgin

Gorda. It became known as "Little Dyk's" which was later changed to Little Dix. Today it is the site of the upscale resort, Rosewood Little Dix Bay (BVI Government, *Our History*).

In the late 17th century (1672) England took control of the BVI. Virgin Gorda was one of the islands that were primarily settled by plantation owners who imported slaves from Africa to work on the cotton and sugar plantations.

Curing House of the Nail Bay Sugar Works

The Nail Bay Sugar Works is one of the Plantation Era Heritage sites and is regarded as the most intact of sugar mills remaining on Virgin Gorda. In the event that your curiosity is piqued, the ruins pictured here are located on the grounds of the Nail Bay Resort.

The Environmental Profile of Virgin Gorda (2012) reveals that by the beginning of the 19th century sugar production had ceased and the population of Virgin Gorda was 102 whites, 130 free coloureds, and 507 slaves. The Virgin Islands Population and Census Housing Report of 2010 showed that 14 percent or 3930 persons resided on Virgin Gorda.

The emancipation of the slaves in 1834 and the granting of full freedom in 1838 ushered in a time of farming for the people of Virgin Gorda as a way to make a living. This way of life was supplemented with fishing and burning of charcoal which was used primarily for cooking. The present economy is highly dependent on tourism which is fervently encouraged and advertised in various publications.

The emancipation of the slaves on August 1, 1834 is recognized and celebrated each year during the first week of August on neighbouring Tortola. Virgin Gordians and people of surrounding islands travel to join in the revelry of Caribbean music, parades with floats including a Queen of the parade, island cuisine and dancing.

Virgin Gorda is a place of beauty, of transition and ongoing development, serving to align it with the more modern aspects of today's world. However, *ole time* sayings and some remaining traditions continue to remind us of a time long ago when things were different – when children played in the street, when doors were not locked, when adults and children sat together and listened to the older folks tell *ole time* stories and sharing was a common practice.

Virgin Gordians have always been a proud and hard-working people, not afraid to make known that they, like the plants and various types of vegetation and animals that are indigenous to the island, were "born here." Unfortunately, with the passage of time many of the *oldies* I knew as a child have been claimed by the cycle of life, leaving the island with a different, but still hard-working demographic.

> *"It matters not where someone is born,*
> *But what they grow to be."*

Inspired by Harry Potter

Source: Google images

Virgin Gorda is relatively small, measuring only eight square miles and is the third largest of the BVI, with Tortola and Anegada coming in first and second, respectively. It is also the second most populated of the islands that form this spectacular archipelago which over time has become a favourite tourist attraction. It is also a destination of choice for many travelers, as well as expatriates who have chosen to call it home.

The topography of the southwestern end of the island is made even more dramatic by the presence of enormous boulders precariously resting on each other throughout the area, both along roadways and in residential areas. Many of these boulders have been given quirky names like Thursday Rock which had little wells that caught water when rain fell and served to quench our thirst when we were in the area; Parson's Rock and Gun Rock....... and there is also the Drowning Rock which, by its very name has an ominous connotation. However, I have no knowledge of the origin of these names or their significance, but as a child I sometimes wondered why they had names as people did.

Weather erosion over time has resulted in irregular and interesting shapes of these mammoth stones and some residents are now incorporating these spectacular creations into the construction of their houses, giving the buildings added appeal.

Road to the Baths

In addition to its gigantic boulders and world-famous beaches, Virgin Gorda is also home to the dwarf gecko, also identified as the Virgin Gorda Dwarf Least Gecko, which was first discovered in 1964 by biologist Richard Thomas on a wooded slope in the vicinity of Pond Bay. It is the smallest known terrestrial vertebrate, measuring about 18 mm (approximately 0.71 inches) and is almost as small as a dime in United States currency, so you can see that Virgin Gorda's fame comes in many shapes and sizes.

As evening approaches, one might occasionally hear a chorus of croaking frogs calling to each other in operatic fashion. This behavior may last throughout the night and is simply one of the many sounds one might hear when living in the islands. Crickets which are nocturnal creatures may also be heard chirping during the night and you might be occasionally treated to the sparkling tiny lights of fireflies in surrounding trees.

Ground lizards are a common sight and may go in and out of an open door with no obvious fear of the inhabitants. It would certainly not be unusual to spy an iguana crawling along the ground or lounging in the trees overhead.

These are regarded as "introduced invasives" by the environmental profile of Virgin Gorda. They remind me of small

Iguana on Long Road

alligators so I am not exactly fond of them. I spied this one on Long Road, in front of our house on a very hot, sunny day. I estimated its length to be about three feet.

Virgin Gorda is home to some of the world's most pristine and unspoiled beaches – The Baths, Spring Bay, Devil's

Bay, Savannah Bay, Pond Bay, Little Dix Bay and several others - some of which have been recognized in the category of "Best Beaches." in the popular upscale travel magazines, Conde Naste Traveler and Travel and Leisure.

The island is endowed with a very scenic coastline and the Copper Mine Point does not disappoint with its craggy stone outcroppings, deep blue water and waves crashing into the wide expanse of jagged rocks.

An added attraction in the landscape of many of the beaches is one of my favourite shrubs, the low-growing, sprawling sea-grape (C. uvifera) plant which produces large bunches of edible grapes. The branches are very sturdy and are placed into graves at the time of burials after the casket has been placed, but before the grave is filled. This custom may sound strange to some readers but I think that the different practices in which the various islands engage only help to add to their enchantment.

Coastline at Copper Mine Point

Sea Grapes (Source: Carol Daniel- Faust@FineArtAmerica)

~*Protected Areas of Interest*~

"The most beautiful rocks have faced the hardest waves."
Kruti J`oshi

The Baths-

On the southern tip of the island lies our most famous beach, the iconic landmark known as The Baths. It was designated as a National Park in 1990 and is regarded as one of the "must-see" attractions on a visit to Virgin Gorda.

This beach is accessible only by boat or on foot. If approaching by foot, one must park at the "Top of the Baths" which is a restaurant and boutique area, then proceed to hike for approximately one mile along a narrow, unpaved path outlined with natural vegetation and boulders of various shapes and sizes.

Care must be exercised when navigating this trail in order to prevent falls and subsequent injury.

Upon arrival at this beach, you realize that the trek was worth every step! One immediately observes that there is a surround of massive grey, granite boulders which rise out of the ocean to form grottoes and upon further examination you discover that there is a maze of tranquil tidal pools that allow for intimate explorations by water enthusiasts. It has been estimated that some of these boulders are as large as forty feet long and the geological placement is simply amazing!

The Baths

This spectacular wonder is majestic in its appearance, its size and general appeal. The reaction of visitors is usually one

of awe and general wonderment! The spectacular formation is believed to be the result of volcanic eruptions thousands of years ago, with the molten lava rock cooling and forming these gigantic granite boulders

The water here, like other beaches on the island, is crystal clear, allowing for snorkeling with up-close views of the amazing marine life below. The waves coming into the surf crash into these huge boulders creating large plumes of white frothy bubbles, providing for beautiful photographic opportunities. The sparkling, clear water under these caves and grottoes is usually warm, being heated by the huge boulders sitting in the blazing sun overhead.

Off to the right of the entrance is the Poor Man's Bar where a variety of cold drinks, including alcoholic ones are available for purchase. At the time of my last visit there, the bar also provided a variety of sandwiches and burgers, just in case hunger pangs set in before you are ready to return to civilization.

Although it is a bar, and just in case you forget to pack your snorkeling gear, you may also find these items there along with life vests and floaties for the little ones. To help you remember your awesome experience at this beach, you will find that t-shirts and tank tops are also available to take back home.

As children we spent many happy hours at this beach playing hide-and-seek among the caves created by the giant boulders, then running to bathe in the clear, warm water. We sometimes buried ourselves in the sand or made sandcastles which were promptly washed away by the waves coming into the surf.

We often walked along the beach looking for sand crabs and seashells which Mother used to create her many projects. Nostalgia sometimes takes me back to this idyllic period of my life. One must have lived it to truly understand and appreciate it.

The *pièce de résistance* of this beach is the main pool which boasts a cathedral-like ceiling formed by the meeting of the boulders and a pathway that leads to other caves. While meandering through these caves one can occasionally catch a glimpse of tiny fish swimming about, as well as small barnacles clinging to the rocks. Openings between the boulders allow sunlight to creep through causing the water to shimmer with an almost magical appearance.

Rock climbing shoes and water shoes are a good investment if contemplating a visit to this beach. It will make your adventure a little easier and much safer. Snorkel gear and cameras could almost be considered mandatory here so that one does not fail to capture the many spectacular views!

The Baths

Another interesting find at The Baths is the pitch apple tree, which is accessed by gingerly climbing up a huge, slanted boulder located just to the left of the main pool. Visitors to The Baths write their names and comments on the large, waxy leaves of this tree leaving proof that they persevered and made it to the top of that boulder.

The Pitch Apple Tree

Navigating one's way through this maze of boulders may at first appear to be a daunting task, but it can be quite adventuresome and is safely accomplished by following an established rope and step system which leads to yet another gorgeous beach just south of The Baths. It is well worth the trek, because at the end, waiting for you, is Devil's Bay. I consider the name a misnomer, as there is nothing devilish about this equally stunning beach, which is also surrounded by huge boulders.

Devil's Bay

The National Parks Trust describes this horseshoe-shaped beach as "picturesque" and it is a description that accurately portrays the beauty of the turquoise, crystal clear water and white sand. It is another in a long line of pristine beaches on this beautiful island.

Like the Baths, this beach can also be accessed after parking your car at the "Top of the Baths" previously mentioned, then taking a twenty-minute hike through dense, natural vegetation to this incredibly beautiful destination.

Upon arrival you immediately see that the effort getting there was well worth it.

You will discover some of the same amazing rock formations that are the hallmark of the nearby Baths. According to the National Parks Trust, at the southern end of this beach is a trail to

Devil's Bay (Source: DestinBradwell@destinationsgallery.com)

Stoney Bay, another beach where the Atlantic waves pummel the coastline, creating a picturesque but somewhat wild appearance according to my research. Seabirds can be seen soaring overhead (2017) – another area for exploration.

Spring Bay – "The Crawl"-

Just to the north of The Baths is Spring Bay, also known as the Crawl by the local people. The water is somewhat shallow here with similar boulders and hidden caves as at the other beaches. This beach is replete with pools and safe climbing rocks. It is also a fantastic place for snorkeling, so it is the perfect venue to learn how to enjoy this amazing water sport.

Of course, a visit to Spring Bay would be incomplete without climbing up on the famous "jumping rock" and taking a thrilling plunge into the warm water below. As children we were fearless as we climbed and jumped.

We spent many happy days at this beach, enjoying the sea while the adults stayed on shore and cooked delicious food for the annual picnics that were held there.

Rock formation at Spring Bay/The Crawl

Spring Bay/The Crawl – Jumping Rock at the left

Copper Mine Point

On the south-eastern tip of the island are the ruins of the historic and prominent landmark, the Copper Mine which was initially mined by the Amerindians and the Spaniards passing through the BVI. According to British Tourism, they were the first Europeans to mine copper here in the early 19th century (Copper Mine, n.d.).

The mine was constructed in 1838 and mined by Cornish miners as well as men of the BVI. It remained active until 1862 when it was abandoned. This was secondary to a decline in the demand for copper as well as escalating costs in Cornwall, England where the minerals were usually shipped after excavation.

The ruins of the original stack, the engine house, and the main building are part of what has also been designated a National Park, so it is now a protected site sitting on an area of 18.4 acres. It has also been voted the Best Historical Hotspot. Extreme caution should be exercised when exploring this area as it is located on a very steep cliff.

The area can be quite treacherous as it is completely open to the elements and subject to all kinds of weather such as hurricanes and the harsh winds blowing off the ocean onto the

Ruins of the Coppermine

cliffs. Vegetation is quite sparse and windblown although the sea grape seems to thrive here. It is mostly rocky terrain that is visible as one explores the area. Again, great care needs to be taken when walking about the site.

Today, copper oxide or verdigris as well as other minerals are still visible on certain areas of the façade of the ruins. Some rock specimens such as malachite and quartz may be found lying loosely around the site.

The Copper Mine is also home to the white-tailed tropicbirds (phaeton lepturus) that build their nests in the crevices of the rocky cliffs by the sea. They can be seen diving from the high cliffs into the ocean below as they forage for marine morsels.

> *"What's old collapses, times change and new life blossoms in the ruins."*
>
> Friedrich Schiller

~Virgin Gorda as I Knew It~

"A table, a chair, a bowl of fruit and a violin; what else does a man need to be happy?"

Albert Einstein

We resided on the south-western half of Virgin Gorda in a village called Spanish Town, which is, according to the Government census divided into the four most populous areas: Princess Quarters, Crab Hill, Handsome Bay and South Valley. The Valley is separated from the northern half of the island known as North Sound by steep, hilly contouring of the land and the population there is considerably smaller. The Sound has become popular as a haven for boaters because of its multiple anchorages and well protected waters.

Gorda Peak is the highest point on the island with a height of 1370 feet. It has also been named a National Park and is home to some endangered plant species, in addition to the Virgin Gorda gecko previously mentioned. My classmates and I, accompanied by our teachers, were taken on several "nature walks" to the top of this hill where we were rewarded with a panoramic view of the surrounding islands, the beauty of which we did not appreciate as children.

The road to the North Sound is now easily traveled because of nicely paved roads, and the area is home to people who have built their houses behind dense shrubbery and boulders, providing them with privacy from prying eyes. When I was a child this road was passable only on foot or by horse trudging along a narrow, uneven, rocky dirt trail.

This was the mode of travel for my late, great uncle, Bregado Flax who was a teacher for many years at the North Sound Elementary School and for whom the Valley School, the Bregado Flax Educational Center has been named......a much-deserved recognition!

As children we did not realize what a challenge this trek was for him and what a shining example of service and dedication his work represented. We only knew that he took this journey in good weather and in bad.

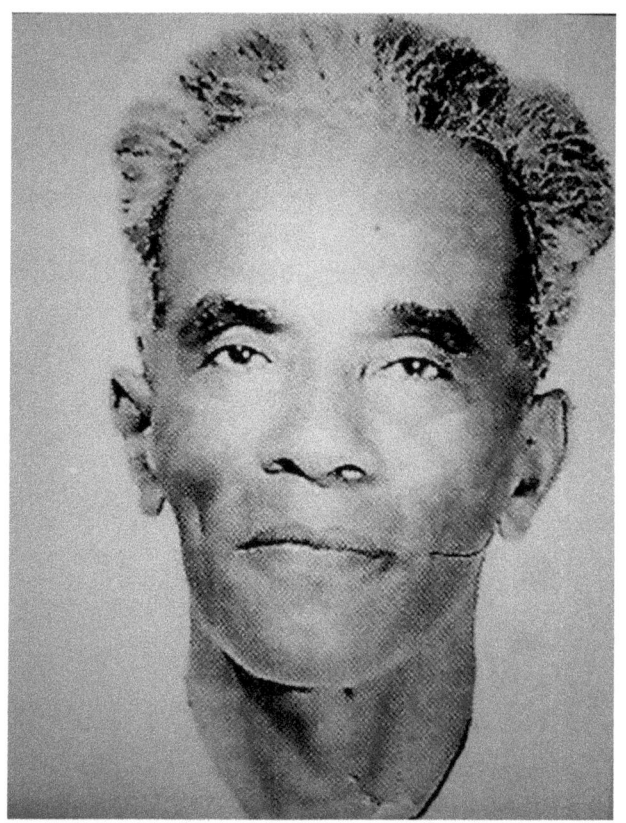

Uncle Bregado Flax – Source: his son, Gerwyn Flax

Uncle Bregado was one of my father's uncles and was married to one of Mother's sisters, Aunt Lily. They lived on Long Road, the same street as we did so we saw each other very often.

On this rainy morning as I lay in bed, the sound of the rain transported me back to the days of my childhood as it so often does. My mind was flooded with memories of tickling my brothers and sister as we hid under the bed sheets from the thunder and lightning, recalling our grandmother, Mamina's ghost stories.

As a result of the rain a new breed of mosquitoes would be hatched in open containers around our property. In a few days they would be ready to extract their daily blood supply from our arms or legs! They were discriminating little creatures as they never seemed to be aware of Mother's presence in the room. Everyone else's bodies were fair game unless you managed to get to them first.

For that, we could always rely on our aunt Lillian, affectionately called Taunie. She was one of Tata's sisters who lived *up the road* and was always ready to save our blood supply from those marauding little pests! She lay in wait for them, always ready to pounce, and as soon as they lit on one of us, she zapped them, frequently with her open palm. Then she announced proudly, "*Ah got he*!" When she was ready to return to her house she always said, "*Ah gone, leave oryuh.*" I think that somehow, they sensed that biting her was a sure death sentence because it appeared that she, like Mother, was also immune to their attacks.

Growing up on Virgin Gorda in the fifties and early sixties represented a time of childish innocence and respect for one's elders. It was as J. R. O'Neal, a relative, said in his memoir, "on Virgin Gorda, life seemed very close to nature…..properties were unfenced. There were no motor vehicles and no electric lights" (2004). It was a time of serenity, a time of unlocked doors, unpaved, uneven dirt roads, latrines or outhouses, kerosene lamps, moonlight walks, Christmas serenades, skipping happily along the road on the way home from school and many other memories that simply bring a smile to my face. It was a time that was unspoiled by modern day conveniences and the rampant commercialism that have become today's norm.

Houses were not numbered and there were no posted street signs. If a stranger needed directions to any given point, he/she would quickly learn that it was all by natural landmarks such as trees or a particular house….."*go down the road and turn right at the corner….when you see the blue house, turn left and then go until you come to the tree with the yellow flowers…make a right and the house you are looking for is the white one on the left."*

It was a world devoid of telephones, television, movies, automobiles, video games and all the distractions that take children away from the truly meaningful things in life. People engaged in intelligent conversations with each other!

There were no stores with *"ready-made"* clothes or frozen foods. The melodious sounds in the environment were those of chirping birds, dogs barking in the distance, the laughter of children playing with each other, the neigh of a horse or the moo of a cow…….and who could forget the *"foreday"* alarm clock, in the form of our rooster that awakened us from the deepest sleep.

Not to be forgotten were the early risers who thought nothing of calling out to say 'Good morning" as they passed by our house, although it was only about six o'clock. Some of them frequently stopped to chat with Tata who liked nothing better.

Mother was also up and "opening the house" because the sun was already "shining"…….it was a no-no to be lying around in bed if the sun was up and shining! It was time to get to work caring for the animals before going to school.

Ours was a world with no social media replete with people being critical of each other or dictating the manner in which one should live. Today's technology was not even a dream. It was indeed an almost utopian life that we lived.

It was a safe, happy place where children could go out to play, away from home without fear that they would be kidnapped

The fowl cock – our alarm clock

or hurt in any way. We often went *down the road* to play with our cousins, Oona, who was the daughter of Taunts Ivy, another of Tata's sisters, and Elody, whom we called Eldie. She was the daughter of Aunt Lily, one of Mother's sisters. When it was time for lunch, or simply time to go home, we were alerted by the shrill sound of Mother's whistle telling us that playtime was over.

It was a time when parents instilled good morals and values in their children and older people were addressed as *Mr.* and *Mrs.* It was a time when children were *seen and not heard.* Conversations among the adults were just that – for the adults. As children we would not even entertain the thought of interrupting or speaking back to our parents when chastised.

Virgin Gorda was simply a dreamy, little island where everyone knew everyone and everyone's animals. We boasted a population of about five to six hundred at the time and we were seemingly sheltered from the ills of the world outside. It was our tropical Eden, teeming with beautiful, fragrant flowers and tasty fruit!

In retrospect, we had little, but it was always enough – yes, we always had everything we needed so we certainly did not consider ourselves poor. We never knew hunger or homelessness or the prejudices that afflict our world today. We were millionaires in our own rights. Yes, we were rich beyond words – rich in ways that could not be measured by money or social classes. We were not "lower class," "middle class" or "upper class." We were just people living harmoniously with each other. We lived a life of contentment. We did whatever our parents wanted us to do and no, we did not receive an "allowance." What was that? We never knew that word!

As individuals we loved and trusted each other and sharing anything we had with our neighbours was a way of life. Sharing was a requirement in our household, and it became one of Mother's life lessons for us. A can of soda was divided into four portions and a piece of candy suffered the same fate, so that each child could have a taste. "You must always share, even if it's just a fly wing," Mother said.

At mealtimes we savoured fresh, home-grown food – now referred to as organic in these more modern times. Mother was the quintessential stay-at-home Mom and ran the household as was customary then, while Tata went to work for the meager wages that made a salary in those days. They were both very industrious and worked very hard to provide for their family. We heard their mantra hundreds of times - everything they did, and everything they owned, was for their children. Although we were not hugged and kissed every day, we "knew" that our parents loved us. They certainly made sacrifices for us in one way or another.

In the process of growing older and reflecting on my childhood, I think that as children we probably thought all of the world's other children lived as we did, because we had no other experiences with which to make a comparison.

Our entertainment came in the form of a Pye radio…..there were no theaters, no stores to buy music or video games. While our parents were certainly not wealthy, they were among the lucky few inhabitants of our island who could afford the "luxury" of this radio that sat on a table with the beautiful lace tablecloth in a corner of the living room.

Each evening we gathered around that radio as a family, to listen to "The Monsoon," an ongoing serial, which we now know as the very addicting soap operas on television. It was amazing how realistic the sound effects were on the radio, and how over time we were able to recognize the voices of the individual actors. These programs were clean with no cuss words or indecent language that have become the accepted norm in present day entertainment. It was lively, fun entertainment that could be enjoyed by even the youngest child, with no need for censorship by parents. Reflecting on that time of my life has cemented one thought in my mind: if given the chance to live my life over, my choice would be to spend my childhood in the same manner as I did in the fifties and early sixties. I wish that my children could have spent their formative years in this type of environment where they could have experienced the ignorance, the simplicity, the innocence and unbridled joy that were the hallmarks of my idyllic childhood.

While my life may have been the same, or similar, had I lived elsewhere, I know that my unblemished childhood on Virgin Gorda and the many wonderful examples of excellent role models with whom I was surrounded, had a profound effect in shaping my character. I have a deeper appreciation of life in general, and a spirituality and trust in God that is rooted in watching my parents kneel together at their bedside to pray. Following suit, we were also taught to say our prayers at night before going to bed and in the morning when we woke.

In exercising the good manners that we were taught, we were expected to address anyone who was in a room when we entered. We said *"good morning"* to our parents at the start of the day and *"good night"* when going to bed.

We read and did our homework sitting at the table with light from the kerosene lamp. We cleaned the glass lampshade or chimney with a soft cloth or piece of paper so that it was crystal clear and provided a nice bright light. We had nothing with which to compare it, but amazingly enough, it appeared to be a very bright light and served the purpose for which it was intended. With the absence of light, we walked the dirt roads on dark nights with lanterns and flashlights to light our way although we knew the location of every stone or jagged rock against which we might bump our toes.

The nights were spectacular when there was a full moon and when there was not, the borderless night sky was illuminated with millions of brilliant stars on an inky, black background. It is one of the most beautiful memories of my childhood. We had so much fun trying to identify the various constellations. Occasionally, we saw a shooting star which we were told was a comet. Because of the absence of electricity on the island, the moon provided the only light that we knew……and oh, what a light it was!

> *"Live in the sunshine*
> *Swim the sea*
> *Drink the wild air"*
>
> Ralph Waldo Emerson

~ *My One-Room Schoolhouse –*
A Dilapidated Shack~

"She had observed that the more education
they got the less they could do.
Their father had gone to a one-room schoolhouse
through the eighth grade ... and he could do anything."

Flannery O'Connor

Our dilapidated one-room schoolhouse accommodated approximately fifty-five of us divided between the first and seventh *standards* as they were called under the British educational system. The younger children wrote on slates with chalk and the older ones used black and white "composition" books.

We went to school at age five, already knowing our ABC's and being able to count as we were taught at home. There were

St. Mary's School – Source: Rose Gardner, my classmate

no kinder-garden or pre-school classes. The first teacher we met was Teacher Ilma who taught the younger children. Our school's construction was entirely of wood with the typical galvanized roof that was common at that time in the islands. It was located to the west of Taylor's Bay adjacent to St. Mary's Anglican Church and was named St. Mary's School.

Our school day got off to a no-nonsense start by our attending Mass in the church sanctuary. I hated the smell of incense and as a little girl I often thought that the priest was going to set the place on fire. There was certainly a lot of smoke! We became well versed in the teachings of the Anglican Church as we learned to genuflect, make the sign of the cross, and say the *Hail*

Mary, a traditional Catholic prayer honouring the Virgin Mary, Mother of Jesus.

At home we had been taught to pray to God, so I never quite understood why we were praying to the Saints and Mary all the time…..and there seemed to be a saint for everything – one for the sick, one for the poor and even one for the animals. I wondered why we never did that in the Methodist Church which we attended but I never asked.

After Mass, we queued up outside to be inspected by our headmaster, Mr. Gunthorpe, who reminded us time and time again that *"cleanliness is next to godliness."* We were required to show our nails and our teeth to demonstrate that we were being diligent in practicing good hygiene. His expectation was that our nails were always neatly trimmed and clean. When he was satisfied that the expected standards were met, we marched into the schoolhouse in a straight line.

Punctuality was not an option but a requirement, and if late, the offending student was not allowed to participate in recess when everyone else went outside to play. The punishment was to sit inside and read a book or whatever work the teacher assigned. Arriving at school repeatedly late or misbehaving in class resulted in the headmaster bringing out his dreaded belt.

The offending children stood in front of the headmaster holding their hands straight out in front so that they were ready to receive the *licks* he mercilessly doled out. Occasionally these licks were given on the back and would sting for a long time. I was on the receiving end of this punishment on one occasion when my friend Nidia (Nidi) and I continued to talk and laugh after we had been admonished to stop. This was quite embarrassing as we were all in one big open room.

Looking out of the windows to the east, we could see big ships and small boats sailing by. I often daydreamed about sailing to far-away places on those ships. I decided that when I became older I would do just that – travel to far-away places. I wondered if people on the ships that appeared close to the horizon could reach out and touch the sky. Oh, the blissful ignorance of childhood!

Our seating arrangement was not one of individual desks and chairs, but instead each class sat at long, wooden desks or tables with long benches. The benches had no cushions, or any type of back support and we were expected to *sit up straight and pay attention* to our teachers' instructions. All the lessons were written on the blackboard with white chalk.

When rain came it brought its own adventure! ……. our rotting roof leaked, and the water also came in through the gaping holes in the sides of the building. This resulted in a quick scramble to move our desks and benches to a dry area until the rain stopped. Of course, this meant that classes were disrupted, and this made us quite happy. Our activity during this time was to sing *rounds* of short choruses such as *Three Blind Mice,* which was an English nursery rhyme and musical round that dated back to the time of King Henry Vlll our teacher said.

> *Three blind mice, three blind mice*
> *See how they run, see how they run*
> *They all ran after the farmer's wife,*
> *Who cut of their tails with a carving knife*
> *Did you ever see such a thing in your life*
> *As three blind mice?*
>
> (Ivemy, 1900)

One of our favourite songs to sing on those rainy days was:

> *"The rain is falling very hard we can't get out to play*
> *But we are happy in the school upon a rainy day*
> *So we clap, clap together, so we clap, clap away,*
> *For this is the way we exercise, upon a rainy day."*

Another wonderful pastime during these rainy periods was the reading of Grimm's fairy tales by the teacher. The modulation of the teacher's voice made the stories come alive and teachers Louis and Eileen noticeably excelled at this. Children frequently interpret things literally, so the one about *Jack and the Beanstalk* always seemed like a mystery to me. I found it puzzling that it was possible for a person to climb on a vine which I thought was like that of the watermelon. Oh, I just marvel at the ignorance and innocence of childhood! It is truly a blissful thing! *Cinderella, Little Red Riding Hood, Hansel and Gretel, Rumpelstiltskin, The Emperor's New Clothes, The Princess and the Pea* and many others were all tales which fascinated us.

There were also Aesop's fables which all had a moral to each story. *The Dog and his Bone* taught us to be satisfied with whatever we had and not be envious of others. *The Hare and the Tortoise* showed that being slow and determined allowed us to achieve our goals. *The Wolf in Sheep's Clothing* stressed that appearances could be deceptive.

Teacher Eileen also taught us about the life of Aesop. She said that he was a slave and storyteller who lived in ancient Greece in 600 BC and that BC meant "before Christ." When we asked if other people lived before Christ, she said that story was for another day. However, she never explained it to us. Aesop's fables were numerous she said, and the vast collection is still available today.

Another *round* which we sang frequently was *Row, Row, Row Your Boat* as we held hands and gently rocked against each

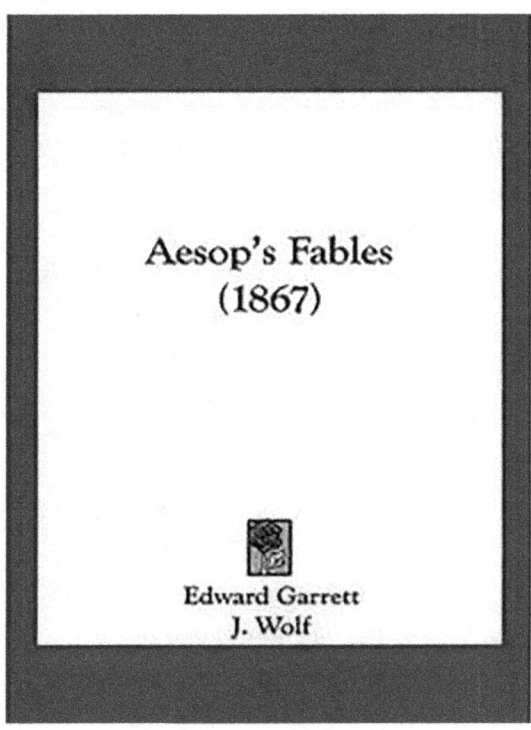

other and giggled, as if we were on a boat. Sometimes it was the only song that we sang continuously until the rain stopped.

> *Row, row, row your boat,*
> *Gently down the stream*
> *Merrily, merrily, merrily, merrily,*
> *Life is but a dream*

(Kubler, 2003)

We learned the poems of the famous poets by repetition. Our teacher read each line of each verse and we repeated them until we had memorized them. My favourites were William Wadsworth's "*I Wandered Lonely as a Cloud."* (Wadsworth, 1802) and Robert Southey's *"The Battle of Blenheim" (Southey,1704).*

I wandered lonely as a cloud
That floats on high o'er vales and hills,
When all at once I saw a crowd,
A host, of golden daffodils;
Beside the lake, beneath the trees,
Fluttering and dancing in the breeze.

Continuous as the stars that shine
And twinkle on the milky way
They stretched in never-ending line
Along the margin of a bay:
Ten thousand saw I at a glance,
Tossing their heads in sprightly dance.

The waves beside them danced; but they
Out-did the sparkling waves in glee:
A poet could not but be gay,
In such a jocund company:
I gazed—and gazed—but little thought
What wealth the show to me had brought:

For oft, when on my couch I lie
In vacant or in pensive mood,
They flash upon that inward eye
Which is the bliss of solitude.
And then my heart with pleasure fills,
And dances with the daffodils.

Sixty years later, I still remember every word of this poem!

As I write these, I realize that these poems are long, and that some readers may just skip them over, but it gives me another chance to indulge in their beauty. I feel as if I am back in the classroom at St. Mary's! Like Wadsworth, I can sometimes close my eyes and "see" the daffodils dancing in the breeze. Oh, what a lovely sight in my mind's eye!

Each of these is beautiful in its own way. While one spoke of pretty flowers, the focus of the other was the questions of small children who had found a skull and asked questions of their grandfather as to its origin. Although many years have passed, I still remember and love these poems.

Source: Children's Encyclopedia

The Battle of Blenheim

It was a summer evening,
Old Kaspar's work was done,
And he before his cottage door
  Was sitting in the sun,
And by him sported on the green
His little grandchild, Wilhelmine.

She saw her brother Peterkin
Roll something large and round,
Which he beside the rivulet
  In playing there had found;
He came to ask what he had found,
That was so large, and smooth, and round.

Old Kaspar took it from the boy,
Who stood expectant by;
And then the old man shook his head,
  And, with a natural sigh,
"'Tis some poor fellow's skull," said he,
"Who fell in the great victory.

"I find them in the garden,
For there's many here about;
And often when I go to plough,
  The ploughshare turns them out!
For many thousand men," said he,
"Were slain in that great victory."

"Now tell us what 'twas all about,"
Young Peterkin, he cries;
And little Wilhelmine looks up
  With wonder-waiting eyes;
"Now tell us all about the war,
And what they fought each other for."

"It was the English," Kaspar cried
"Who put the French to rout;
But what they fought each other for,
I could not well make out;
But everybody said," quoth he,
"That 'twas a famous victory.

"My father lived at Blenheim then,
Yon little stream hard by;
They burnt his dwelling to the ground,
And he was forced to fly;
So with his wife and child he fled,
Nor had he where to rest his head.

"With fire and sword, the country round
Was wasted far and wide,
And many a childing mother then,
And new-born baby died;
But things like that, you know, must be
At every famous victory.

"They say it was a shocking sight
After the field was won;
For many thousand bodies here
Lay rotting in the sun;
But things like that, you know, must be
After a famous victory.

"Great praise the Duke of Marlbro' won,
And our good Prince Eugene."
"Why, 'twas a very wicked thing!"
Said little Wilhelmine.
"Nay... nay... my little girl," quoth he,
"It was a famous victory.

> "And everybody praised the Duke
> Who this great fight did win."
> "But what good came of it at last?"
> Quoth little Peterkin.
> "Why that I cannot tell," said he,
> "But 'twas a famous victory."

As children we did not pay a lot of attention to the story of the poem, but we were all quite fascinated with the discovery of the skulls. We learned all the Christmas carols in the same manner although sometimes they were written on the blackboard.

School concerts were a favourite event and they always featured a play that was the main attraction of the program.

Each student's role was handwritten on several sheets of paper by our teacher. We dutifully memorized our lines, and we rehearsed the play multiple times until our teacher was satisfied that we had the correct pronunciation of all words and that we knew our entrances and exits. My favourite of all the plays was the one in which I played the part of the main character, *The Lady of Stavoren*.

As I made my entrance, all cast members shouted loudly "*Make way for the Lady of Starvoren*", "*Make way for the Lady of Starvoren*" as they cleared the path with their hands. I felt so special in the pretty dress that Mother had lovingly made for the occasion!

Our teacher said that it was a Dutch folk story written many centuries before about a young, rich widow who lived in the Netherlands in Europe. (Statues of the Lady in Europe today show her looking out to sea as she awaited the arrival of her merchant ships with more riches).

Penmanship was a subject in itself. The teacher wrote a proverb or some famous quote on the blackboard with all the letters and loops perfectly spaced between the lines that had been drawn on the board. The expectation was that we would copy this proverb exactly as it was written, being sure that our loops crossed on the line. Perfection was expected and if our loops were not perfect, we were required to repeat them until they were.

In the process, we developed beautiful penmanship and learned many proverbs or adages which I did not previously understand. As time passed, and with patient explanation by Teacher Louis, I understood what *"A bird in the hand is worth two in the bush"* meant and *"A rolling stone gathers no moss"* finally made sense.

We learned to write with fountain pens which were filled with liquid ink and we also used stick pens with nibs that we dipped into little inkwells built into our desks. No pencils and erasers for us! This dilapidated, leaky one-room schoolhouse was a beehive of activity and learning. With no worldly distractions we were extremely focused on our lessons and self-discipline was always the order of the day.

No current fashion, jewelry or hairstyles for us! My classmate Nidia and I often competed to see which one of us would achieve the highest grade on a test. In this British educational system, we did not have the luxury of multiple-choice examinations. The answers to all questions were written in essay form, so you either knew the answers or you did not.

On Friday afternoons, our headmaster, Mr. Phipps, introduced us to classical music which we listened to for at least one hour. He taught us about the great masters and their compositions and in the process, we learned all about Johann Strauss and Pyotr Ilyic Tchaikovsky. Amazingly, we even learned to spell and pronounce their names!

We became little experts in the lives of Sebastian Bach and Ludwig van Beethoven and listened to the works of Wolfgang Amadeus Mozart as well as the water music of George Friedric Handel.

Over time we learned to dislike all of them, their music and our headmaster. We thought it was all very boring and wondered why it was necessary to listen to the music of dead people when we could instead listen to the modern songs that were being sung on the radio by Paul Anka, Bobby Vee and others. Our headmaster insisted that music appreciation was important for us to learn and we would appreciate it as we grew older.

I appreciated his insight at age eighteen when I discovered that I immediately recognized various classical selections when I heard them and came to the realization that it was the kind of music I most often enjoyed listening to. I subsequently purchased several long-playing records (LP's) of the masters which are still an integral part of my music collection today. As I enjoy this music now that I am older, I have a deep admiration for my headmaster and his efforts to instill in us an appreciation of the Arts in this dilapidated one-room schoolhouse.

Another headmaster, Mr. Christopher, assigned us silly topics on which we were instructed to write essays. The one topic that I remember after so many years is the ludicrous title *"It Was Nothing but a Rat in a Tin."* He also wrote a play which he titled *"The Fussy Flower Garden."*

He insisted that he was simply assisting us in the development of our *creative* abilities. We, on the other hand, thought he was crazier than his essay topics. Some years ago, I was able to sit with Mr. Christopher on a visit to Tortola and reminisce about those days and those silly essays. It was also an opportunity for me to give him the credit for my passionate love of writing. He told me "You were always my best student." Even so many years later, I still appreciated hearing him say that and it is a compliment that I will always treasure.

Friday afternoon was game time. We established two teams which competed skillfully in a game of *rounders* which is the same as the United States national pastime known as baseball. We did not appreciate it then, but I ask myself now, how many children go to recess and play games with the ocean a stone's throw away? It was an idyllic childhood that we had and one which is forever gone. I savour with great joy my fantastically wonderful memories!

A favourite activity in which we frequently indulged during recess was to lie on the green grass and roll down the hill on the sloping part of the field. Then we lay on our backs and looked up at the clouds, while we tried to determine what their shapes resembled. We gave no thought to our clothes becoming rumpled or stained with the grass. Even now, as these memories flood my mind, they bring a big smile to my face. It was just pure, clean fun!

Another major event in our school lives was the celebration of the birthday of Queen Victoria on Empire Day, May 24th, although she was no longer alive. The festivities began with the national anthem, *God save the King* in deference to King George who was the reigning monarch at the time. It was mandatory for us to stand at attention, looking straight ahead as we sang of our allegiance to His Majesty. After his death, we honoured his daughter, Queen Elizabeth ll in the same manner.

The remainder of the day consisted of bag races in which the contestant stood inside a burlap sack with a rope tied around his/her waist and hopped to the finish line. In the three-legged races two children stood with their arms around each other while the right leg of one and the left leg of the other were tied together as they attempted to run as fast as they could to be winners. The egg race had competitors who ran while balancing an egg in a spoon, and of course there were lots of food, drinks and dancing. These were wonderful times for everyone, children and parents alike, full of merriment and laughter – again, a time of ignorance and innocence - a time of unadulterated fun and fellowship - a time of love and trust – a time when all the values and traditions we held dear were cherished and honoured.

St. Mary's School may have been little more than a shack, but I learned many valuable lessons there. I am called upon occasionally to verify for my co-workers the number of days in any given month. They look at me in amazement when I recite this little verse. Didn't everyone learn this in elementary school? Not so apparently. I take great pride in reciting for them the English mnemonic rhyme which was used to differentiate between the number of days in the Julian and Gregorian calendars.

Thirty days hath September,
April, June and November
all the rest have thirty-one
excepting February alone,
which has but twenty -eight days clear
and twenty-nine in each leap year.

(Grafton,1562)

…..and who can forget the whimsical nursery rhymes that we learned with such gusto!

Baa, Baa Black Sheep, have you any wool?
Yes sir, yes sir, three bags full.
One for the master and one for the dame
and one for the little boy who lives down the lane.

Of course, there were many others including *London Bridge is Falling Down, Falling down, Humpty Dumpty sat on a wall* and Mary, Mary Quite Contrary, how does your garden grow? One of our favourites:

> *Ladybird, ladybird, fly away home*
> *Your house is on fire, your children all gone*
> *All except one, and her name is Ann*
> *And she hid under the frying pan.*

(Cooper, 1744)

These days when I speak about learning my *times* tables, I usually have to explain that I am referring to multiplication tables, and if I speak of *cursive* handwriting, I find that not many people know to what I refer. I am convinced that braving the rain and thunder and lightning in that leaky one-room schoolhouse year after year, instilled in us better coping skills than people who were more fortunate than we were.

As at home, morals, values and discipline were instilled into our young lives, helping to set the foundation on which we would build our future ones.

> **"A teacher affects eternity.**
> **He can never tell where his influence stops."**

Henry Adams

> *"The influence of teachers*
> *extends beyond the classroom,*
> *well into the future."*

F. Sionil Jose

~House of My Childhood~

*"Honour the house in which you were born,
the tree that gave you shade,
and the village where you were raised."*

Swedish Proverb

The house in which I entered this world and where many of my childhood memories were also born was bought by Tata, my father, from his mother whom we called Mamina. It was a two-room house constructed entirely of wood with the living room and dining area in the front part of the house and a bedroom in the back. The bedroom furniture consisted of two beds and a crib. My parents occupied one bed, my older brother and I shared the other bed and the baby slept in the crib which Tata skillfully constructed as our family grew. Five of us slept together in one room and we were all as happy as clams.

Ellsworth, Mother and Maizie

We did not enjoy the luxury of a bathroom or a kitchen. Lack of a refrigerator meant that there was no ice and drinks were consumed at room temperature.

When Mother was pregnant and went into labour, we heard her moaning as we waited in the living room while Tata left to bring

Miss Iris, the midwife, to the bedside. Because transportation was on foot, it took a little time for him to return. While my brother slept in the rocking chair, I listened to Mother moaning and I wondered how long it would be before the *bawbaw* was born. After Tata returned, I listened quietly as Miss Iris gave him instructions to boil water. She spoke very softly to Mother while she attended her so I could never tell what was going on except for Mother's moans.

Then, suddenly there was the shrill cry of the *bawbaw* who sounded annoyed to have been disturbed. Shortly thereafter, Miss Iris would take us into the bedroom to see Mother and the new baby. New babies always smelled so good!

It was customary in those days for a new mother to be confined to bed for eight to ten days and the midwife made daily trips to care for her and the baby. There were no bottles of formula then. Mothers lovingly *nursed* or breastfed their babies, and gradually they were weaned to bottles filled with cow's milk. There were no monthly visits to the doctor for newborn shots, or vitamins as children got older. Amazingly enough, children simply thrived on fresh cow's milk, home grown foods and an unending supply of their parents' love and attention. There was obvious bonding between mother and child in those early days. As children became older, there was no real open demonstration of affection between parent and child, no constant hugging or kissing, but we all instinctively knew that we were loved without question.

In the bedroom was Mother's *trunk* in which she kept new nightgowns in case she became *sick* and it was also there that she kept the new clothes she had made for the baby while she was pregnant. That was how we knew we would be having a new baby brother or sister – mother would start sewing little clothes. In those days though, the word *pregnant* seemed to be taboo. Women were referred to as being *in the way* when they were expecting, and although they were anxious to get rid of *the burden*, they were thrilled when the new baby arrived. There were no prenatal visits or vitamins or ultrasounds that are routinely done in these more modern times.

It was during one of these times when Mother was in bed with the new baby, that I learned how to fry fish. Tata's culinary skills were sorely lacking, so at eight years of age, I became the designated chief cook and bottle-washer for our family while Mother was indisposed with the new baby, my sister, Maizie.

I remember carrying a dish with raw fish into the bedroom, where Mother showed me how to make slits or *jags* on both sides of the fish, and season them by putting the salt and pepper into each little jag. She taught me from her bed, how to heat the pot, then put in the lard and fry the fish until they were browned on one side and then to turn them so that the other side could also be nice and brown. She instructed me to be careful so as not to burn myself. Everything was cooked with lard! After the fish was fried, I returned to the bedroom with them, so that Mother could inspect them and tell me if they were done properly.

While Mother was indisposed, I swept the floors and polished the furniture, and served food to Mother, Tata and my brother, Keith. I cleaned the dishes, and I swept the dirt yard with a bush broom. A bush broom was made by gathering several branches of the *marorn* tree which were held together with a piece of twine. I felt very grown up that I could do these things that Mother usually did.

Our house was surrounded by Mother's beautiful garden which she lovingly tended and for which she won "Best Garden" awards throughout the years as the Agricultural Department held their annual Exhibition events. There was an abundance of flowering plants including bougainvillea and oleander in a variety of colors, jasmine, roses, ixora and perennials - zinnias, bachelor's buttons and coxcomb, which filled the air with the fragrance of their tropical blooms.

There were assorted ferns – lace ferns, maidenhair ferns and silver ferns which had a silver powder on the back of the fronds. We often pressed the fronds against our skin so that we could see the pattern created by the fronds. The vibrant colors of assorted crotons and coleus (Joseph's coat) added their own splendor to the landscape.

Normally, food were cooked in a coal-pot which was used for that purpose throughout the Caribbean islands. It was an urn-shaped iron device which held a grid inside, on which charcoal was placed. The charcoal was lit and the pot with food was placed on top and cooked slowly. An opening on the side of the coal-pot allowed the wind to fan the flames of the fire and

Traditional coal pot

cause the charcoal to burn quite efficiently. It helped to know in which direction the wind was blowing. If there were no wind Mother would take an old hat and fan the fire until the coals were blazing hot.

Because we had only this cozy two-room house, the coal-pot was used outside. As time passed, Tata built Mother a kitchen which was not attached to the house – an architectural design that presented a few problems but was common practice in the islands at that time. Mother's nephew Berris, who was a very skilled mason, crafted the walls with the beautiful granite stone that Tata loved and had collected for this purpose.

He had gathered them over time and our faithful donkey, Jenny, had dutifully carried the loads from out South to our house. Ken, my younger brother at the time had followed along carrying one rock which was securely nestled in the *cotta* on his little head. He went everywhere with Tata.

Berris patiently chiseled away at the stones until he achieved the desired shape and then expertly fit them into the appropriate grooves before applying the mortar to hold them in place.

In bad weather, morning or night, Mother sprinted from the kitchen to the house with a jacket covering her head, and our food in her hands. We gathered around the table with two benches which were in one corner of the living room and ate lunch which was the big meal of the day. We always ate together as a family.

As our family grew, so did our house. Tata constructed a dining room in the space between the kitchen and the living room, a second bedroom and a bathroom with a tub, a shower and a sink, but no toilet., so we continued to use the outhouse.

Prior to having that bathroom, we bathed in the bedroom in a metal tub we called a *badin'pan*. It was not a large pan, but somehow, we managed to fit our bodies into it and luxuriate in our baths!

It was the same pan in which Mother washed our clothes, gently scrubbing them on the washboard, then clipping them to the clothesline with clothespins so that they could dry. The white clothes were washed with a big chunk of *blue* which was a chalk-like substance that prevented the dingy, yellowish film which eventually formed on white clothes. The blue made everything sparkling white.

When clothes were removed from the clothesline, they always smelled very fresh from billowing in the clean air which was devoid of smog or other pollutants. Ironing the clothes was another process: the iron or "goose" was filled with charcoal and turned in the direction of the wind to heat up the coal. Clothes were sprinkled with water prior to ironing as it helped to get

The badin pan

wrinkles out. White shirts and any other items that needed a little stiffness were "starched" with a concoction of flour and water. This mixture was boiled and cooled, then the clothes were immersed and hung out to dry.

Since we did not have the luxury of hot running water, Mother boiled water in a big kettle and mixed it with cold water to make a warm bath. Most of our water came from the rain, but we also retrieved water from the public pump well as needed. We carried a pail of water on our heads using a cotta.

At bath time one of us children would bathe first, then the other would get into the same water and amazingly we felt clean

The Goose

when we got out. The thought never occurred to us to ask for fresh water. This was how we lived....if it was good for one of us, then it was good for all of us. Sometimes I asked Mother, *"Why do I feel so good after I take a bath?"* Her response was always the same, *"because you washed the dirt off."*

Necessity made for some unconventional practices in our lives, some of which included brushing our teeth with bath soap or ground charcoal ...after all, there were no stores to run out to and buy toothpaste. I can safely say that my childhood was one of unparalleled adventure!

Going to the restroom was another story – another adventure in the middle of the night! We had no indoor plumbing on the island, so everyone had an outhouse or *latrine* on their property. I hated them because of the horrendous smell that was almost unbearable. If one of us needed to go the toilet at night, we woke a brother or sister to go outside in the dark with us. No one ever complained about any of this – it was just what we did – it was how we lived. If we just needed to *pee-pee,* or urinate, we used *the chamber pot, or poachie*, which was kept under the bed for that purpose, ready to be used as needed. In the morning it was emptied and cleaned so that it was ready for the next night.

Mother was a very skilled seamstress who designed and made all our clothes – *frocks*, skirts and blouses for my sister and me. When the school year started after vacation, all of us children had a whole new wardrobe that Mother had lovingly made during the summer. Mother bought fabric in St. Thomas for only twenty-nine cents per yard, she later told us.

Girls and women wore only frocks and the men and boys wore *pantaloons*. The men were the only ones who literally wore *the pants in the family*. She also made the clothes my brothers wore, as well as the sheets and pillowcases on our beds. The white cotton bags which held about twenty pounds of flour were not tossed aside when empty.

Nothing was ever wasted. Those bags were washed and ironed and became pillowcases which were stuffed with snowy, white silk cotton. The pods of silk cotton were produced by the tree which grew on our property. It was a family affair to sit and remove all the seeds from this beautiful white product that was so soft and silky, before our pillows were stuffed with it. It was blissful to rest our heads on those pillows at night. Mother frequently taught us *"waste not, want not."*

Throughout our childhood we were reminded to share and to avoid waste. We participated in all family activities whether it was gathering eggs or feeding the animals. A sense of responsibility was something we learned at a very young age - we learned that along with taking, we were also expected to give of ourselves in one way or another.

> *"All of us remember the home of our childhood. Interestingly, our thoughts do not dwell on whether the house was large or small, the neighborhood fashionable or downtrodden. Rather, we delight in the experiences we shared as a family. The home is the laboratory of our lives, and what we learn there largely determines what we do when we leave there."*
>
> Thomas S. Monson

~Mother – A Woman of Strength Unfailing~

"A Mother's love is something no one can explain.
It is made of deep devotion and sacrifice and pain.
It is endless and unselfish and enduring come what may,
For nothing can destroy it or take that love away"

Helen Steiner Rice

The photograph below is my favourite one of my parents. I look at it and I see their love for each other.

I see commitment and an intimacy they alone share.

I see that they are dressed in their church clothes, so this tells me that they have come home from church services which they never fail to attend, even in inclement weather.

God takes center stage in their lives – they have complete trust in Him.

Mother and Tata

Mother dislikes being photographed but she is smiling in this one, as she gazes lovingly at the man she loves so much, and Tata looks as if he is falling in love all over again!

They are momentarily in a world of their own, in a committed, loving relationship, in a marriage that lasted for 58 years before God called him home.

Mother was born on East End, Tortola and made frequent trips to Virgin Gorda to help her sister Lily with her babies. This is how she met and married Tata and made Virgin Gorda her home. Aunt Iva, Aunt Violet and Uncle Hugh were her siblings who lived on East End and whom we saw from time to time.

At the writing of this book, Mother is five months away from her one hundredth birthday and I praise God that she is still able to move with the aid of her walker, and most importantly, she still knows all of us. She is an amazing woman who insists that as long her legs can move, she is moving! Her strength and determination know no bounds. One of my best memories of her is as a younger woman with her long straight hair styled in *plats*. I wish she could live forever, but of course that is wishful thinking. I live seven thousand miles away from her, but I think of her every day and I thank God for allowing me to be born to her.

Mother was a kind, loving person who did not pry into anyone's business and avoided getting into any *mele`* or *strumoo*. She used to say, "I only know what you tell me." She was the glue, as is so often the case in families, which held ours together. She cooked and cleaned and washed and saved for *a rainy day*. These days she bemoans the fact that children are not being nurtured by their mothers, or are not being gently carried, or their little hands are not being held. It makes her unhappy to see little ones running to keep up with their fast-walking parents or to hear parents cussing at their children. Mother would never be guilty of this behaviour.

As I said before, we had no form of transportation on Virgin Gorda. Imagine living in a place with absolutely no vehicles! Imagine the open roads where one could just stroll and stop to chat with a friend. Imagine the quiet and solitude with the only sounds being those of people talking, chimes blowing in the wind, birds chirping or a dog barking in the distance. Such was our experience on this virgin island, untouched by progress and where everyone was truly the other's neighbour.

This idyllic lifestyle was marred only by my running into a barbed wire fenced with my eyes closed as we happily skipped along the road on the way home from school. My left knee bears the scar but even now, after so many years, when I see that scar it brings a smile to my face as I remember that it represents a special time during my happy childhood days.

We were all quite physically fit because our only option was to walk everywhere we needed to go. We walked to the Methodist Church over to the north with Mother carrying the baby and holding the hand of the youngest child. If it were a hot, sunny day then she had the oldest child, me, hold the hand of my brother and she would carry an umbrella over the baby. This routine was repeated every Sunday because we never missed going to church.

Sunday was a day for praising God, and we refrained from singing any secular songs. We carried fresh-cut flowers from Mother's garden and placed them on the graves of our sister, Dahlia and our brother, Ken every Sunday morning before going to church. Mother taught us to sit quietly in church and listen to what the minister said. She said it was not a place to misbehave, but a time to worship God. Again, discipline!

We always dressed up in our Sunday best which Mother had lovingly sewn on her Singer machine and we always wore hats. Our hair had beautiful curls which had been created in a special way: we cut strips of brown paper which we then twisted and placed at the end of a hair section and rolled until it could not be rolled anymore; we then tied the ends of the twisted paper and slept with our "curlers" overnight. In the morning we had curls that we were proud of!

After the worship service was over, we went home for lunch. After eating we went *down the road* to buy "specials" from Miss Charlotte, who was May May's maid. Specials were nothing more than flavored, sweetened water that had been poured into an ice cube tray and frozen (May May had a refrigerator by this time). We quickly ran back to our house before the specials melted and we all enjoyed this Sunday afternoon treat! Sometimes we had sugar cakes which Mother made from grated coconuts. Occasionally she made them look different by adding a little food coloring and then they were a pretty pink color, or sometimes they were brown if she cooked the coconut with brown sugar.

At three o'clock we walked back to the church to attend Sunday school. Each Sunday school attendance was recorded in our individual books with a little red star which was stamped by our teacher. At the end of the year, we each had fifty-two stars because we never missed a day of Sunday school. One of my favourite memories of Sunday school was singing the immensely popular children's hymn:

> *Jesus loves me! this I know,*
> *For the Bible tells me so.*
> *Little ones to Him belong;*
> *They are weak but He is strong.*
>
> *Yes, Jesus loves me!*
> *Yes, Jesus loves me!*
> *Yes, Jesus loves me!*
> *The Bible tells me so.*
>
> (Warner, 1860)

A fun church activity we did as children was going door to door with our assigned coin folders soliciting donations for missionaries abroad. The folders held nickels, dimes and quarters. Our goal was to fill the folders and present them in church on Missionary Sunday. Even then, as children we were taught the importance of sharing and giving to help others although they were far away, and we did not know them personally.

The church event that I liked best was our Harvest Sunday program. The service began with the singing of the harvest hymn:

> *"Come ye thankful people, come.*
> *Raise the song of harvest home*
> *All is safely gathered in*
> *Ere the winter storms begin*
> *God our Maker doth provide*

> *For our wants to be supplied*
> *Come to God's own temple, come*
> *Raise the song of harvest home"*

While the hymn was being sung, both children and adults processed in with trays piled high with colourful fruits and vegetables – the bounty of the harvest – in addition to cakes, tarts and sugar cakes. These were all laid at the foot of the altar while the minister prayed and thanked God for the bounty that supplied our daily needs. Later that afternoon or early the next morning, this bounty was sold to raise money for the church and for missionary needs.

During those years of my childhood, I thought Mother could do everything. She used her incredibly talented hands to create various objects of beauty. She cut and glued *"carto"* boxes of various shapes which she covered with tiny shells we had collected in the sand when we went *in the sea*. We did not say that we were going to the beach. She outlined mirrors and picture frames with these same shells, creating her own designs as she went along. These masterpieces were displayed around our house for all to see. Similar items selling in stores today are not inexpensive.

She crocheted doilies and other table coverings as well as lace collars with which she enhanced her dresses. She never used any pre-made patterns but when she completed a project it was a beauty to behold. Our house was as well dressed as we all were.

Her intricate, embroidered scallops were found on the edges of sleeves as well as beautiful flowers on little hand towels.

On one of my recent visits to Mother she gave me some of those towels which I will always treasure. She made beautiful table runners with a type of time-consuming embroidery known as faggotting which was accomplished by pulling out horizontal threads from the fabric and tying the remaining threads into groups to form little posts. Her imagination and creativity seemed to know no bounds!

Mother was a *Jill-of-all-trades*. On the western side of our house was a large patch of sisal, also known as the snake plant and mother-in-law's tongue. From time to time Mother cut blades of this plant and scraped them with a knife in a vertical direction until the underlying threads were exposed. Afterward she rinsed them with water until they were white and then she hung them on the clothesline to dry. It was fascinating as a young girl to watch Mother take several strands of these threads and manipulate them into flowers and leaves of various designs and create the most beautiful placemats on which she sometimes created embroidery. There was no end to her creativity.

Mother

She also dabbled in hairpin lace and teneriffe lace which is a needle lace that originated on the island of Tenerife, the largest of the Canary Islands. How did Mother get this knowledge or develop this art? She was always creating something. She took leaves from the branches of the coconut tree and scored them into little strips which she interlaced to make very practical placemats. She also shared this art with the women of her church during the summer while Vacation Bible School was in progress.

These same strips were also sometimes braided into long flat ropes which were then sewn on the ever-present Singer machine in such a fashion as to create a wide brimmed hat which Tata used when he worked in the pasture with the animals.

Smaller hats were created for us, the children, and while the male hats got just a plaid or solid color band around the crown, my sister's and mine had a beautiful ribbon or piece of fabric tied into a bow. Mother was so adept at making these hats on her machine that people on the island placed orders for hats.

The most striking hat Mother ever made was one of clear cellophane. I never knew the origin of the cellophane, but she thought that it should not be discarded, so in the process, a very fancy church hat was created. She was ingenious! She said we should never waste anything, and as a result she made use of everything. *"Waste not, want not,"* was the mantra with which she frequently admonished us.

Mother designed and sewed all our clothes. My sister's and mine had fancy frills and lace-trimmed Peter Pan collars, multiple rows of tucks, puffed sleeves and beautiful sashes for tying in back. She saw to it that we had ribbons or barrettes in our hair and that we wore our *anklets*, which were socks with a little lace-trimmed cuff that was turned down. She was an accomplished seamstress who also occasionally designed and made wedding gowns for women in our community.

Looking at us no one could ever call us poor, thanks to Mother and her talented hands which were always creating something. Mother believed that it was important to save. "*Even if it's only five cents it will add up*," she told us. Tata always praised Mother for being the financial guru of our household, even if the amount was small. She managed it all quite well and there were always a few dollars hidden away for a *rainy day*. Of course, in those days, we were able to go next door to Miss Ethel who had a *shop* in one room of her house, and buy 5 cents sugar, flour or lard. The amount was more than enough to make several loaves of bread.

Mother's bread was the best home-made bread anyone ever tasted! One of my unforgettable memories of home is the smell of hot bread with melting butter. As I write, I can almost smell the bread being baked! I watched Mother make yeast bread and cover them up for a while to *sweat,* after which she kneaded them again before placing them in the well-greased and floured pans before baking. She made sweet bread with raisins, as well as

Old brick oven

guava, coconut and guava-berry tarts at holidays and other times in between. She baked all these decadently delicious items in an oven at least fifty feet from the house. The oven was constructed of brick and mortar and was big enough to hold several tarts at the same time.

Just like the coal pot, the oven had a little vent on the side to allow the coals to heat up. When the oven was hot, the coals were removed or moved to the side and the vent was closed to trap the heat inside. The bread and tarts were placed in the hot oven using a baker's peel. Mother always knew when it was time to take them out and they were perfect every time! Mother's tarts had the flakiest, best tasting crusts anywhere. She never measured any ingredients when she baked but instead, she just looked at the amounts with a skilled eye. The finished products were always done to perfection.

For many years after we all went abroad to school, Mother sent us each three tarts at Christmas, so that even though we were far away, we could continue to enjoy her delicious baked goods.

Another creation of Mother's that no one else seemed to be able to match was her *mauby,* which is a bittersweet drink made from the bark of the mauby tree. She added anise, cinnamon, orange peel and a combination of various herbs and leaves to make *leaven* which she then combined with a sugar-water mix a day or so later. I never tire of drinking this drink and even tried to imitate her recipe once, but my resulting mixture could not remotely compare with Mother's. She made mauby at night before going to bed and poured it into several bottles. In the morning, because of the fermentation from the leaven, each bottle had several inches of white froth/foam coming out of the top of the bottle and curling down the side. This indicated that the mauby was ready for drinking.

Mother insisted that we share everything with each other. Drinking a can of juice or soda before it was divided into equal portions was not an option. She continually reminded us, *"even if it's a fly wing, you must share it."* As young children have a tendency to do, I took everything literally, and I wondered why anyone would eat a fly wing. I did not understand that Mother was teaching us a lifelong lesson which has served me well. It was a trait which I instilled into my own children many years later.

She made guava-berry, our traditional island drink at Christmas and poured it into a pretty glass decanter which she placed on the table for visitors to share. The production of guava-berry was a process which took a few months. The berries were placed in a giant glass bottle known as a demijohn and steeped in rum. Sometime before Christmas, Mother made syrup of sugar and water with whole stick cinnamon and other spices and poured into the demijohn with the alcoholic mixture. I am not sure if there were any other ingredients since I have never made this drink myself. The guava-berry drink took on the dark red color of the berries and is a hallmark of Christmas celebration in the islands. Christmas would not be Christmas without it! In fact, when the serenaders came on Christmas day to play their beautiful music, they played this song:

> *"Good mornin, good mornin,*
> *ah come for de guava-berry."*

On Christmas Eve night Mother "cleaned" and then boiled a whole ham which came in a cloth bag. It was then placed on the table so that everyone, family or friends, could all enjoy it when they stopped by on Christmas Day.

It was a special time when people visited each other, sharing all the decadent foods of the season. It was a time of merriment and laughter with everyone wishing each other the greetings of the season.

The commercialism which has now become rampant with each holiday was absent. It was a time when everyone remembered the true meaning of Christmas and dressed in their best clothes to go to church and celebrate the birthday of the baby Jesus. Guava-berry and ham, tarts, cakes, fruitcakes, and another drink known as sorrel were some of the delicacies that everyone enjoyed and shared with each other. Sharing was not something we thought about – it was simply something we did. For us, it was a way of life.

Mother could be called a doting wife as she was extremely attentive to Tata. Some of my fondest memories of the two of them together are of Tata lying on the floor with his head in Mother's lap, while she combed his hair. Sometimes she brought a basin of water and *washed* his hair, then put on a little hair grease and a *stocking cap* which was made by cutting off the top of an unwanted stocking and making a knot at the narrow end. This cap would stay in place for several hours or overnight and would keep the hair in perfect condition.

Additionally, Mother would sometimes bring soap and water in a basin to the table for Tata to wash his mouth and his hands after eating fish. Yes, she spoiled him, and he enjoyed every minute of it!

I remember being upset with Mother (and Tata) because I was not allowed to go to dances at the Community Center while my brother, Keith could attend. Mother said I could not go to every event, because people had names for girls who were *always on the street.* I thought it was simply not fair. Still, she was the more lenient of my two parents.

A special time with Mother was when we all went *in the sea.* She was probably the best swimmer on Virgin Gorda and as children we were fascinated as we watched her dive and float.

She taught several of the children on the island to swim, but I just did not master it well, so my swimming skills are still quite deficient. We carried lots of mangos in the sea with us and dipped them in the saltwater as we ate them. They somehow seemed to taste better when we did that.

Another fond memory is our visits to Aunt Iva and Aunt Conce who lived on East End, Tortola. Getting there was an adventure in itself as travel was by sailboat. Because the boat had no engine, the captain was dependent on the wind direction and had to "*tack*" about.

This is a sailing maneuver which allowed the captain to guide the boat into the wind and be propelled along. A trip that now takes thirty minutes was about four hours or longer in those days with some passengers experiencing seasickness. In retrospect, the wind was an important element in our lives.

Aunt Iva and Aunt Conce were Mother's sister and aunt. We, the children and Mother, visited for a couple of days and though we never called it a vacation, I suppose that is what it was. Aunt Conce was blind, but somehow, she always knew when we entered the room. As a child, I did not understand that her other senses had become more acute because of her blindness.

Aunt Conce (deceased)

We loved to climb up on her four-poster bed which I thought was the most beautiful bed I had ever seen. I enjoyed visiting with our other cousins who lived on East End, and seeing Uncle Hugh who was Mother's brother, and his wife Aunt Rosalind. They never came to Virgin Gorda, so this was our only hope of seeing them.

As a child I did not appreciate it, but as I grew older, I developed a great sense of admiration for Mother's inner strength and trust in God. She taught me to pray and believe and be patient, because as she put it, *"God may take seven years to answer, but he will answer when the time is right."* I hoped in some situations throughout my life that he would answer my prayers a little more expeditiously!

Mother was a woman who endured the unspeakable – she buried three of her seven children, one after another, and kept her sanity! A few years ago, when I asked her how she survived those ordeals, she replied that she *"prayed a lot."* The poignancy of these events will be addressed in a later chapter dedicated to my siblings.

I quickly learned that her faith in God was her secret weapon for overcoming life's obstacles. It was her Rock. She was always very thankful for what she had, even if it were little. There was no competition to keep up with the Joneses! She taught us to be content with whatever God had blessed us with and not to envy what other people had – her belief in the tenth commandment.

This sentiment though, was a prevailing foundation of life in the islands. People trusted in their God from deep within their souls and believed that he would take care of them. They did not worry about tomorrow. They did not concern themselves with the lack of anything, because they prayed about any and everything and they just *knew* that God would provide for them. Unwavering faith, contentment and a sharing spirit lived in the islands.

In school we were taught to locate the Ten Commandments in the twentieth chapter of the book of Exodus. We memorized them and could be called upon at any time to differentiate between them. We were taught to live by those rules. We learned the names of all the Books of the Bible – yes, all sixty-six of them, and again, could name them all in chronological fashion on the spur of the moment.

The Beatitudes in the Gospel of Matthew, Chapter 5 were taught to us as the beginning of the Sermon on the Mount. Again, we memorized these verses and could recite them correctly without any advance notice. The Ten Commandments, the Books of the Bible and the Beatitudes were considered important lessons for us, as children to know. This was easy because we were not distracted by television, telephones and social media.

The central activities of our lives were attending school and church and helping with the animals as well as the *ground*. This was the place where we grew *provisions* that consisted of potatoes, yams, pigeon peas, watermelons and the like. We were happy, carefree children who were truly blessed with the innocence of childhood – Mother made sure of it.

We sometimes played board games such as Monopoly or Chutes and Ladders, but mostly we played Chinese Checkers. Mother was a master at this game, and it was a rare occurrence for anyone else to win. Still, we enjoyed watching her strategize her moves.

"Love as powerful as your Mother's
leaves its own mark.
To have been loved so deeply
Will give us some protection forever."

J.K. Rowling

~Reading – A Family Affair~

"What an astonishing thing a book is.
It's a flat object made from a tree with flexible parts
on which are imprinted lots of funny dark squiggles.
But one glance at it and you're inside the mind of another person."

Carl Sagan

Mother and Tata were both avid readers, so there was no shortage of books around our house. They both seemed to be always reading something. As a child my favourite book was our school textbook known as the Nelson West Indian Reader. However, Mother was the one who frequently gathered us around her and vividly retold the stories she had read. She read classics such as *Uncle Tom's Cabin* which very graphically detailed the horror and brutality of slavery in the early nineteenth century.

We learned all about Uncle Tom who was a faithful and pious slave. He was beaten to death by his owner, but as he lay dying, he prayed for his master who treated him so poorly to repent and be saved. Sometimes Mother seemed sad when she told us of these horrors, yet our curiosity was piqued, and we wanted to hear more. We learned about the slave-owner's daughter, Little Eva, who was white but treated the slaves with kindness.

Source: Personal Collection

Mother always pointed out that the stories she shared with us all had a lesson to be learned. In this story, she said, everyone deserved to be treated kindly, regardless of their station in life.

Mother also read *The Silver Chalice* which told about a Greek silversmith named Basil, who was commissioned to sculpt an outside holder for the cup which Jesus used at the Last Supper. Mother showed us the picture of the chalice with the beautifully etched faces of Jesus and his disciples around the rim of the silver cup. In retelling this story, Mother also told us of Jesus and his last evening with his disciples in the Upper Room. Just as Jesus shared bread with them, Mother again reminded us of the importance of sharing what we had with others.

Our favourite story, and one which Mother told many times, was *The Basket of Flowers*. It was about a girl named Mary who grew up in a beautiful cottage with her father, James who was a very godly man and a gardener. He taught her the importance of humility, honesty and forgiveness. Their idyllic life was interrupted when Mary was falsely accused, tried and convicted of the theft of a diamond ring. She was sentenced to death, but Mary insisted on her innocence.

Mary remembered that her father taught her that *"it is better to die for the truth than to live for a lie, and that the worst pillow to sleep on is the pillow of a guilty conscience!"*

During a storm when a tree branch broke, the ring was discovered, and it was determined that the ring had been snatched through an open window by a magpie that was attracted by its glitter and had taken it to its nest. Mary was vindicated. Mother said this story showed the importance of telling the truth, regardless of the consequences.

The book that our parents read most often was the Holy Bible. In fact, in later years, Mother scheduled five o'clock in the afternoon as her designated time to read the Scriptures. Nothing else would happen during that time. She read and really focused as she read. She read only the King James Version. She said that other versions did not appeal to her – they did not seem like the Bible, she said. This version is still my favourite one.

While listening to a broadcast on our Pye radio, I heard a program which involved memorizing fifty Bible verses and having a parent or sometime confirm that this was done. After completing this exercise, the appropriate signed form was returned to the Bible Crusade in Oklahoma and I was awarded my very own Bible with my name printed on the cover. I was sixteen years old. I still use this Bible today although over the years it has become quite beaten up, in need of a trip to the bookbinder. However, it serves the purpose.

Several years ago, my Tata noticed that it was falling apart, and he spent some time taping it together in his masterful way until I could get it repaired. Now that he is gone, I have decided not to have it fixed – the tape is a reminder of his love and patience in fixing it for me.

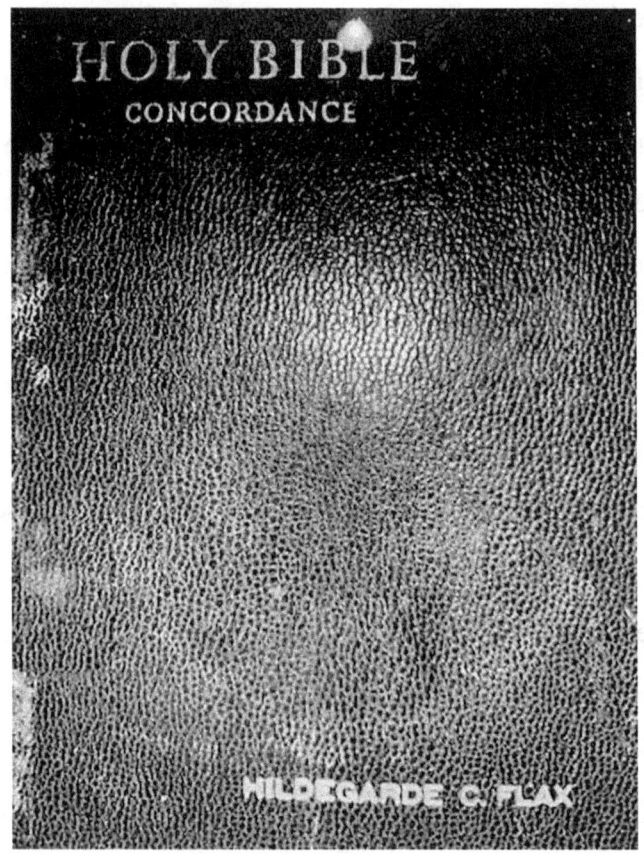

My Bible

On Her Wedding Morn was another of Mother's favourite stories – it was a romantic novel about the joy of marrying someone you love – it was also sedate enough to be shared with her children.

They were all such lovely stories and all of them with lessons to be learned. As was typical of that time, stories were clean and could be enjoyed by even the littlest member of the family.

The names our parents chose for us came from the many books they read. Consequently, we all have uncommon names with wonderful meanings. The origins are as follows:

My name – **Hildegarde Cilicia:**
Meaning: warrior or battle stronghold, province
Origin: Hildegarde (German) and Cilicia (Latin)

As Mother told us, when she was a young woman and not yet married, she read a book titled *The Blue Window*. This was the love story of Hildegarde and Krispin. She was apparently quite impressed with the character of the heroine in the book and decided that if she ever married and had a daughter, she would name that child Hildegarde. Several years ago, after an exhaustive book search, I obtained a copy of this book and was pleased to discover that the person in the book and I, are remarkably similar in character. I told myself that Mother had chosen well! My Biblical middle name was bestowed upon me by Tata and is found in the 22nd chapter of the Book of Acts in the Holy Bible. Cilicia is the name of a city and was the birthplace of St. Paul the apostle.

My older brother – **Keith Lancelot**

Meaning: forest, servant

Origin: Keith (Celtic or English), Lancelot (French)

Keith's middle name was chosen by Tata. It appears that Tata had a penchant for choosing middle names! Literature tells us that Lancelot was the most trusted of King Arthur's knights in the well-known classic, the *Knights of the Round Table*.

My only sister – **Maizie Euridice**

Meaning: Pearl, broad justice

Origin: Maizie (Gaelic or Scottish), Euridice (Greek)

Maizie's middle name derives from Greek mythology which identifies Euridice as one of the daughters of Apollo, the God of Light. Maizie was also the name of Mother's friend.

My younger brother – **Ellsworth Tennyson**

Meaning: nobleman's estate, God of wine

Origin: Ellsworth (English), Tennyson (Greek)

Ellsworth's name was chosen after I introduced Tata to the work of another poet we had learned about in school, Alfred Lord Tennyson. Tata read one of his poems, *The Charge of the Light Brigade* and he said, "I like that name "Tennyson." Ellsworth's middle name was born!

> *"What's in a name?*
> *That which we call a rose by any other name*
> *Would smell as sweet."*
>
> William Shakespeare

My parents were well read – fiction, non-fiction, Greek mythology, poetry, novels and other works, in addition to the Holy Bible - as is evidenced by the quality of their reading material and the origins of our names. No John or Mary or Robert for any of us! I give them both the credit for my voracious love of reading.

> *"I feel the need of reading.*
> *It is a loss to a man not to have grown up among books."*
>
> Abraham Lincoln

~Gastronomic Delights~

> *"True gastronomy is making the most of what is available, however modest."*
>
> Claudia Rosen

The food we ate as children was always fresh and prepared daily. *Leftovers* were never found in our household and we did not take lunch to school or work. In retrospect we were probably some of the healthiest people in the world. All our food was organic – although we never referred to it as such and it was lovingly grown by the entire family or made from *scratch*. No additives or preservatives for us!

No one became ill except for an occasional cold which was quickly remedied by some *bush tea* which was a bitter concoction cooked up by Mamina, our paternal grandmother who lived a couple of houses away, down the road. My brother Ellsworth still enjoys his personal blends today – one of which is a delicious combination of rock balsam, mint and lemongrass, equally enjoyable, hot or cold.

Growing produce/provisions and livestock was the mainstay of our island, so families planted and harvested their own crops and raised their own animals. We had a *ground* or garden in which we planted sweet potatoes, pigeon peas, watermelon, muskmelon (cantaloupe), cassava and eggplant which we called *boulanjay*.

Tata's Grafted Mango

We also planted okra and banana trees, guavas and mangoes. This was a family affair, so when it was time to reap the results of our hard labour we all got down on our knees, literally, to dig for sweet potatoes. We shelled pigeon peas together and gathered buckets of mangoes as well. There was nothing to compare to the sweet taste of the grafted mangoes that Tata grew.

We raised sheep and goats, cows and fowl (adult hens and roosters). Among this menagerie of animals were one donkey, one horse, one dog, one hog and one duck. As a child, I never thought of our property as a farm, but many years later when my children visited, they were delighted to be on the "farm" as they referred to it. They were fascinated with the big hog which they promptly named *Arnold* after the same animal on the television show, *Green Acres*. Our "Arnold" was really a girl hog who had a litter of eight or ten pigs which would later become *corned pork*.

Although Tata had built a chicken coop, the hens were allowed to roam free during the day. Mother would usually *"feel"* them to determine if they were going to lay eggs that day. If that were the case, a piece of string was tied to the hen's leg and this was a way to keep track of its whereabouts. We sometimes discovered a nest full of eggs which would be gathered up before the hen had time to nest on them and turn them into little chickens.

Occasionally, there were eggs that were not found in time and they eventually hatched. It was delightful to see eight or ten little yellow chicks following along with their Mother who clucked and fussed over them and guarded them as though they were the most precious things in the world. I think it is safe to assume that being *protective like a mother hen* had its origins in that behaviour. We fed these little ones with cornmeal that had been mixed with a small amount of water.

Sometimes we had the opportunity to witness the birth of a chicken as the eggshell cracked and we watched with amazement as the little chick pecked its way into the world, leaving the safety of its shell to venture into the unknown. It was all wet and ugly, but after a few minutes under its mother's wing, it was dry and a bright, fluffy yellow color. Yes, there is nothing to compare to a Mother's love and nurturing.

When the chickens matured, they were sometimes sacrificed to make Mother's delicious *chicken pilau* in which the chicken was combined with rice and different spices and then cooked as a single dish. I have never been able to replicate Mother's way of cooking it, so I really enjoy it on my visits to her. Unfortunately, the absence of grocery stores on our little undeveloped island made raising animals for food a necessary element to our survival.

Corned pork and dumplings were a favourite delicacy. The pork was cured by pouring large amounts of salt into big gashes made in the meat, after which it was hung on a line to dry for several days, much as washed clothes were hung out to dry. When cooked, it was served with flour dumplings and perhaps a piece of tannia, which is a starchy root and a staple of Caribbean food. It remains a decadent dish which I enjoy whenever it is available on my visit to the islands. In retrospect, our meals were high in carbohydrates as it was not unusual to have peas and rice, green bananas, sweet potatoes or tannia on the same plate.

Salt fish is simply salted cod, which was also served with flour dumplings and perhaps fried plantains. When she was able, Mother cooked it for me on my visits home. The fish is boiled several times and the water poured off to eliminate some of the salt. It is then sautéed with onions, tomatoes, garlic, pepper and any other seasoning or spice of choice. *Peas and rice* accompanied many of our dishes.

Okra fungi is another dish that I love and is a traditional British Virgin Islands recipe. It is made of cornmeal with chopped okra incorporated into the mix. Lots of butter goes into making this delicious side dish which can be molded onto a plate, taking the shape of whatever it has been poured into. Historically, fungi can be traced back to the days of slavery when each slave was allowed by Danish law to have six quarts of Indian meal and six salt herring on a weekly basis.

Dobe meat was usually made from beef and was extremely tasty. I never learned what went into making this dish, but I remember that the meat was dark brown. In watching the women cook this dish at picnics on the beach I learned that brown sugar was sprinkled into the hot, melted lard before the meat was put in. There was a slight sweetness to this dish which always made it very tasty.

Fried plantains were a staple and accompanied most meals as a side dish. The riper the plantains, the sweeter they were, so Mother waited until the outside skins were almost black and soft. This is still one of my favourite things to eat with any meat or chicken, or even just on a slice of bread.

Of all the foods Mother cooked for us, the one I liked best was *pea soup*. It was usually made with pigeon peas or kidney beans which we called *red peas*. It took a long time to cook the peas, so Mother started cooking them early in the morning. She added lots of sweet potatoes, dumplings, tannia and salted pig tail which enhanced the flavour. Also added were fresh chibble (green onions or scallions) and thyme leaves. She incorporated sugar while the soup was cooking, so that it was slightly sweet when it was finished. I still put sugar in *all* my soups, even if they are not made with peas or beans.

Fried fish usually consisted of doctor fish, yellow tail, cororn, snapper, king fish and old wife, which is my favourite fish. There were also cavalli, mackerel and bonito which were known as *seine* fish because they were caught in a net. Sometimes we even enjoyed lobster and shellfish which always reminded me of a little box with its almost square shape. The lobster and shellfish meat were lightly fried or sautéed with onions, tomatoes, Worcestershire sauce and garlic. Sometimes Mother boiled the fish and served it with an incredible white sauce which I later learned was simply a combination of mayonnaise and butter.

We occasionally had fish soup which was just as delicious with its many dumplings and sweet potatoes. Mother also made some wonderful *fish cakes* which she created with fish, flour, chopped onions and whatever else she wanted, then fried. We wasted nothing and when we ate fried fish, we ate the entire fish including the eyes. As children, we found sucking out the eyes of the fish to be quite delightful. Even now, I find it amusing!

Whelks and rice were another delicacy we enjoyed often. Adults and children would *pick* buckets of whelks off the sea rocks bordering the bay near Fort Point and take them home in anticipation of a delicious meal. It was in this same area that we picked the mamee fruit off the trees in between the sea rocks.

The whelk is a marine gastropod which resembles a snail and has been referred to as a *sea snail*. The whelks were boiled for a period of time until they would be easily removed from the shell. This was accomplished by gently knocking the shell against a hard surface or grabbing the meat with a fork or a knife. The whelks and rice were then cooked together as one dish, and was oh, so delicious!

Our big meal of the day occurred at lunch time and we walked home from school every day to eat the hot food that was waiting for us. We all had lunch at the same time. Breakfast was called *tea,* and anything eaten in the evening was also referred to as tea. Breakfast consisted of bread and egg, bread and cheese, or oats (hot oatmeal) cooked with whole milk, raisins, freshly grated nutmeg and brown sugar. Sometimes we had cream of wheat instead, also cooked with whole milk, fresh from our cows. An occasional treat was *guinea corn pap,* a delicious hot cereal which was made from ground guinea corn. *Tea* was black tea, coffee or Ovaltine. Having tea was simply having breakfast or something very light in the evening.

Because of the lack of electricity on the island, we also had no refrigerators. Milk was boiled and used the same day. To create a special delicacy which, in retrospect, does not sound appetizing, a portion of the fresh milk was set aside in a calabash. The calabash was made from half of a scooped-out gourd-like fruit which grew on a tree in our yard.

After several days of the milk sitting at room temperature, the top was covered with a thick cream which was scooped off. The remainder of the milk had soured and coagulated into big white clumps with a pale, yellow liquid. This separation of raw milk is known as curds and whey. We sweetened these clumps with sugar and ate them. We called it *bunniclawer.* It was one of our favourite things to eat. Is this what Little Muffet ate in the nursery rhyme?

> *Little Miss Muffet sat on a tuffet*
> *Eating her curds and whey*
> *Along came a spider*
> *Who sat down beside her*
> *And frightened Miss Muffet away*

(Gilbert, etal. 1877)

It is said that Little Miss Muffet's name was Patience and that she was really the daughter of Dr. Muffet who was an entomologist (a person who studies insects) in the 16th century. One day while Patience was eating breakfast, one of Dr. Muffet's spiders frightened her and she ran away.

The cream that had been set aside was used to make freshly *churned butter,* not with a butter churn, but simply by shaking. The cream was poured into a jar with salted water and after the cover was securely in place, the shaking process began. I do not remember how long this lasted, but after a period of vigorously shaking the jar, the cream was replaced with clumps of fresh butter floating in the water. This freshly made butter had a similar taste to the Danish butter which we occasionally bought in St. Thomas. It did great justice to Mother's hot bread.

Mother made the best *macaroni and cheese* which was cooked in milk so that it was very creamy. The thing I liked best about this dish was that she sprinkled raisins in it while it was baking. Perhaps this is where my love of raisins started as I also cook my macaroni and cheese with raisins.

I do not think that Mother ever made *souse,* but we bought it from Miss Charlotte just down the road. Souse was made from the hog's head and ears, knuckles and sometimes the shoulder. I think that perhaps the feet were also added. It was spicy hot and very tasty though it does not sound particularly appetizing. Blood pudding, as it implies, was made from the hog's blood and was another spicy delicacy that many of us enjoyed, but Mother never made it and so, I never learned how.

Of course, I cannot talk about our many delicacies without mentioning *johnny cakes*. They were made from flour, water, baking powder, salt and a dash of sugar and kneaded until smooth. Mother cut the dough into small squares or rounds and fried them in hot lard. They were mouth-watering good and were eaten with our *tea* or maybe with fried fish. Everything was fried with lard which came in big blocks of a pound or more. We never used any of the various cooking oils that are used today.

I would be remiss if I did not talk about the various goat dishes we enjoyed. Nothing was wasted as I have previously noted. *Head and foot soup and tripe* were two that we really enjoyed. Tripe was the intestinal part of the goat and does not sound at all appetizing, but it was. It took some time, but Mother would take as long as was necessary to clean those parts very well before cooking.

These soups were full of tannia, sweet potatoes and dumplings. We also enjoyed *bull foot soup* which was made from the feet of the cow. All these soups were highly seasoned with different spices and herbs including fresh chibble and thyme. Going home to the Virgin Islands is always more special if I can savour any of these delicacies of my childhood.

"Bon Appétit"

- Julia Child

~Superstitions, Ghosts and Jumbies~

*"The graves stood tenantless, and the sheeted dead
Did squeak and gibber in the Roman streets."*

William Shakespeare, Hamlet

Mamina, whose name was Eloise, was our paternal grandmother who also lived on our street, Long Road. Unfortunately, my maternal grandparents were deceased before I came along.

Mamina had a flock of goats and sheep which she tended in the southeastern part of our village in a wilderness of bushes, but she always knew, like a good shepherd, if one of her flock was missing and she would search the bushes for it. As I think about it now, I do not know how she navigated her way through the forest of wild trees, but she did. By the time she made it home, it was dark outside as she meandered through the narrow, rocky path that was the road to home.

She usually stopped at our house for *tea* and frequently as she tarried for a while, the conversation gravitated to the ghost and *jumbie* stories and *ole time tales*. We loved to hear them even though they scared us half to death and we were afraid to go to sleep. The tales were frequently about others who had died long ago but were seen by some people *walking the earth without any feet* and vanishing completely as the living person got closer. She would tell of seeing someone walking in front of her, but she could never catch up to that person even though she walked faster, and then the person would suddenly no longer be there. Sounded rather spooky!

There were stories of huge piles of salt disappearing into thin air! Sometimes the ghost was allegedly a recognized relative who came back to give much needed advice before going away as quickly as he or she had come. These stories were so fascinating that we all believed every word to be true because our Mamina would certainly not tell a lie.

Uncle Bregado was another source of these ghost stories. The one thing we did not like about him as children was that he smoked a pipe, and we hated the way it smelled, but he was just as good a storyteller as Mamina was.

There were tales of hearing someone cough or speak when no one was there, and that would frequently be taken as an omen that perhaps that person was going to die soon.

If a folded sheet or tablecloth was opened and a triangular crease was noted in the middle where all the folds came together, it would be interpreted as indicating a coffin, signaling the death of someone in the family.

Sometimes a bird flew into the house and this was most certainly a harbinger of a death to come. No one ever thought that the bird had lost its way! A certain level of sadness prevailed for a time, knowing that someone we knew was going to leave this earth. Because we had no telephones and no way to communicate news other than in person, the tolling of the church bell was an announcement that someone had passed away.

Bad luck would certainly ensue if an umbrella were opened in the house, or if the floor were swept after dusk. If one stepped out backwards through a door, he or she would *carry someone out* – that is, someone in the house would die. An itching foot meant that you would soon walk on someone's grave dirt. If the big toe was *"biting"* or itching, surely someone was going to die. You could almost sit and wait for the news because it would come. I must confess that I believe this one to be true.

Most of the superstitions seemed to be related to death, but there were others which heralded good things to come. Itching of the *right hand* meant that one would receive money. Call me silly and superstitious for sure, but I believe in this one because I always seem to receive money when my hand itches. I never think that perhaps my skin is dry and simply needs a little lotion! If the *left hand* itched, it denoted spending of your money.

If while combing your hair, you dropped the comb, it meant that someone somewhere was writing you a letter which you would soon receive. If the hem of your dress were upturned, you could expect to get a new dress. If the *right knee* itched, it was an indication that someone was going to sleep in the house, that is, a visitor. The itching of the *left knee* signified that a member of the household would sleep out and itching of the elbow signaled disappointment of some kind.

It is only with the writing of this book that I realize how important this particular superstition of itching was in our lives. Twitching of the *right eye* meant that one would cry and twitching of the *left eye* brought lots of laughter and joy.

If a woman were pregnant or *in the way* and craved or disliked a certain food and touched her body, the baby would have a birthmark of that food when it was born. I know of someone who disliked doctor fish during her pregnancy, and her daughter was born with a big, dark mark, the size of a doctor fish on her back. Now, is that superstition or a generous collection of melanin in that one spot?

Walking under a ladder was certain to bring a streak of bad luck and if one pointed at someone's grave, the offending finger would fall off! A shoe that was turned upside down would result in your Mother's death. If someone talked about how well things were going in his life, he would quickly tap his knuckles on the table or anything that was wooden and close by, saying *"lemme knock on wood"* as a precaution. This would ensure that the good things would continue for him.

Newborn babies had an open Bible placed by their heads to protect them by warding off any evil spirits lurking in the wind. If a baby had hiccups, a sign of the cross on the forehead with the mother's saliva or *spittle* was a sure cure.

Children were not allowed to drink coffee because it would make their heads *hard* and deter the learning process. However, as a girl of five or so, I sometimes went with Mother up the road to Miss Etma's house (she was the mother of Taunie), and I would drink a little coffee with them. I venture to say that I was the exception to the rule because I had no difficulty learning anything.

Occasionally someone would stop by to visit, but that person would stay for so long a time that all interest was lost in the conversation and in fact, you just wanted him or her to leave. To accomplish this feat, according to another superstition, all one had to do was take a broom, turn it upside down in a corner and sprinkle a generous helping of salt in the broom. Pretty soon the offending person would be gone, and everyone could breathe a sigh of relief.

When the New Moon appeared in the sky it was customary to hold up a piece of silver currency to it. This was intended to bring good luck and prevent one from being broke. When Tata saw the New Moon for the first time in the lunar cycle, he usually called out to Mother to bring him a quarter so that he could continue this tradition. If the moon were upturned enough to hang a bucket on the end, we could expect rain at some time. Tata was my source for these superstitions about the moon. Even now, many years later, I remember him when I see the New Moon and I can hear him calling out to Mother as I look for my own piece of silver in keeping with the customs of my childhood.

>*"A black cat crossing your path signifies that the animal is going somewhere"*
>
>Groucho Marx

~Christmases Past~

*"What if Christmas, he thought,
doesn't come from a store.
What if Christmas, perhaps,
means a little bit more?"*

Dr Seuss, *How the Grinch Stole Christmas*

Christmas was, and is still my favourite holiday. I loved everything about this time of year – the amazing story of Jesus' birth, the beauty of home-made decorations, the sounds of bells, singing of Christmas carols and the aroma of tarts baking or a ham being prepared. It was just a wonderful time of the year for us children, and the high point was the arrival of Santa Claus which we looked forward to with great anticipation.

Christmas meant that we had a program at church, and we all had our roles in the Christmas play which we had so diligently memorized and rehearsed. The church was decorated with a Christmas tree which was really a fishing rod tree with thorns. Because of the lack of electricity, we adorned the tree with tiny candles which we stuck on the individual thorns of the tree. They were lit at the last minute, so that they would last for the duration of the program. Of course, there were lots of melted candle drippings under the tree when everything was done. Each child received a gift which was usually something practical, such as a bar of soap, pencils or a black and white exercise book to be used in the classroom at school.

At home, we had the same kind of tree, but as we waited for Santa Claus, we prepared a little differently to receive our gifts. We did not enjoy the luxury of Christmas stockings *hung by the chimney with care*, as in the old traditional Christmas poem. Our stockings were the big burlap mail sacks in which the mail came to our house because Tata was the postmaster, among other things. Our *stockings* were eagerly hung by the living room windows, one of which was left slightly open so that Santa would be able to enter the house.

During the early evening on Christmas Eve, we were serenaded by a roving band of musicians who visited each house to sing a few Christmas carols before moving on. Uncle Bregado skillfully played his flute, Mr. Allan who was the husband of

Miss Iris, the midwife, created heavenly notes on his accordion, someone played a mouthorgan and Ernest and his banjo as well as maracas also added to the harmonious blending of musical notes celebrating the season. There were some musicians with homemade instruments created from dried out gourd or large sardine cans. We all stood at the open windows in the living room and sang along with them, Tata sometimes chiming in with his own harmonica. At the end of the rendition Mother gave them a donation of twenty-five or fifty cents as a token of appreciation for the wonderful music. Although this does not seem like very much it was a significant donation in those days.

During the entire Christmas season, our Pye radio on the table in the corner of the living room played all the carols that we knew so well. We sang along with great anticipation as the *big day* drew closer. In the week prior to Christmas, I also sang with a group of carolers from our church and we went door to door belting out Christmas carols!

Several weeks earlier, we sat at the dining table and addressed and mailed Christmas cards to family and friends, near and far. I had developed an excellent penmanship, so I was always excited when Mother and Tata allowed me to address some of the envelopes.

On Christmas Eve, while we were being serenaded and anticipation was running high, out in the kitchen there was a whole ham in the pot being prepared for consumption the next day. Mother had already *cleaned* it of all the fat and whatever else needed to be removed before cooking. There is just nothing to compare to the enticing smell of a ham boiling on the fire on Christmas Eve! All the tarts had been baked, and the annual fruit cake which had been ordered from the Sears catalog had already arrived. Tata's favourite candy, *darling creams* were in residence as well as an assortment of other mixed, hard candy. All the preparations assured that everything would be ready for the feast on Christmas Day when we would gorge ourselves with one delicacy or another.

Tata went to midnight Mass at the Anglican Church where he was a member. We were encouraged to go to bed so that Santa Claus could come. If we did not, he would not! At least, that is what Mother told us. As I got older, Aunt Lily stopped by our house to take me to service with her at the Methodist Church at 5 o'clock on Christmas morning. The first hymn that we sang from the hymnal was always the same and I loved it with all my heart:

"Christians awake, salute the happy morn
Whereon the Savior of the world was born
Rise to adore the majesty of love

> *Which hosts of angels chanted from above*
> *With them the joyful tidings first begun*
> *Of God incarnate and the Virgin's son."*

Several weeks before Christmas we always looked at the toys which were so beautifully advertised in the big Eaton's of Canada catalog and vocalized our wishes about what we wanted Santa to bring for us. The children from Crab Hill made fun of us at school because we truly believed that there was a Santa Claus, and they did not. They insisted that our parents put out the gifts after we went to bed. We had many significant arguments about this and would not back down an inch. I think that one of the most beautiful examples of pure childhood innocence is the unshaken belief in a real Santa Claus.

We woke early in the morning and went into the living room to check our burlap *stockings* to see if Santa Claus had indeed come. We were always delighted to find that he brought exactly the things we were hoping for. Certainly, our parents did not put those gifts there – they were sleeping, just as we were. We brought our gifts into the bedroom and Mother and Tata were always very surprised and delighted to see all the wonderful things we had received from Santa Claus. They said that obviously we had been good boys and girls.

A popular toy at the time was the humming top which was made of tin or aluminum which we called *tinnen* and was painted with vivid colors. Its shape was spherical and the stand on the bottom allowed it to be perfectly balanced when placed on the floor.

The pull-out handle at the top was pumped up and down causing the top to spin slowly for quite a while as it hummed the most melodic tune. My top had a merry –go-round pattern of horses on poles all around. It is a little beaten up, but sometimes nostalgia sets in and I get it out of the closet and spend a little time reliving my childhood days. I am so grateful to Mother for

My old Humming Top

putting away some of my gifts from that time of life and even more grateful that every now and then I can once more enjoy them.

On one of those Christmases so long ago, Santa also brought me a xylophone which was a flat musical instrument with individual slats painted in bright colors. When the slats were hit with the two accompanying hammers, it created beautiful high-pitched music that was quite melodious. It was not long before I had mastered the art of playing my xylophone.

There was also the little china tea set I received from Santa when I was eight years old. After I went away to school several years later, Mother kept it safely in her china cabinet and I retrieved it years later to place in my own cabinet after

My doll's tea set

I married. That set is much older today consisting of three cups, three saucers, a sugar bowl, a creamer, a teapot, all of which are prettily painted with blue and orange flowers. The set is missing only one cup and saucer.

My granddaughter, Vanessa, fell in love with it when she was just a little girl and it was displayed in my living room. When she visited, she immediately made a beeline for it and pretended to have her own tea party so, it will go to her when she acquires her own china cabinet.

What child could ever forget the game of jacks with the little red balls? It was one of the games that brought us the greatest pleasure and none of us ever seemed to get tired or bored playing it.

Jacks

Of course, we all knew how to play marbles. They were pretty, round glass balls which were lined up and shot with another marble. The key in shooting the marble was to be able to manipulate the marble between the thumb and the first two fingers and shoot it just right. Oh, the joys of our unblemished childhood! Sometimes I wish that we could go back in time and savour those moments all over again.

Many years into my childhood, and many arguments later with the Crab Hill children, I was disappointed to discover that Santa Claus was not who we thought he was and that he was indeed, our parents. They had paid attention when we pointed out the toys we liked in the Eaton's of Canada catalog.

One year, several weeks prior to Christmas, I found an invoice from Eaton's hidden behind a picture and imagine my surprise when I read it and discovered that the items listed were the same toys we hoped Santa would bring us. Suddenly I realized that the children at school had been telling the truth all along.

I kept this bit of knowledge to myself but waited patiently to see what Santa would bring us that year. Of course, when we checked our *stockings* all our gifts were the ones listed on the invoice. I never revealed my discovery to anyone, but after that, a little of my childhood excitement about Christmas was gone. Many years later Mother shared with me that after they made the purchase from the Eaton's catalog, they kept the toys at Miss Ethel's house next door so that we would not accidentally find them. They retrieved them after we had gone to bed on Christmas Eve.

Another favourite activity at Christmastime was looking into Mamina's View-master and seeing three dimensional views of the various scenes described in the traditional Christmas poem which we recited in school every year. We could hardly wait our turn!

'Twas the Night before Christmas

'Twas the night before Christmas, when all through the house
Not a creature was stirring, not even a mouse.
The stockings were hung by the chimney with care,
In hopes that St. Nicholas soon would be there;
The children were nestled all snug in their beds,

While visions of sugarplums danced in their heads;
And mamma in her 'kerchief, and I in my cap,
Had just settled down for a long winter's nap,
When out on the lawn there arose such a clatter,
I sprang from the bed to see what was the matter.

Away to the window I flew like a flash,
Tore open the shutters and threw up the sash.
The moon on the breast of the new-fallen snow
Gave the luster of mid-day to objects below,
When, what to my wondering eyes should appear,

But a miniature sleigh, and eight tiny reindeer,
With a little old driver, so lively and quick,
I knew in a moment it must be St. Nick.
More rapid than eagles his coursers they came,
And he whistled, and shouted, and called them by name
"Now, DASHER! now, DANCER! now, PRANCER and VIXEN!
On, COMET! on CUPID! on, DONNER and BLITZEN!
To the top of the porch! to the top of the wall! Now
dash away! Dash away! dash away all!"

As dry leaves that before the wild hurricane fly,
When they meet with an obstacle, mount to the sky,
So up to the house-top the coursers they flew,
With the sleigh full of toys, and St. Nicholas too.
And then, in a twinkling, I heard on the roof the
prancing and pawing of each little hoof.

As I drew in my hand, and was turning around,
Down the chimney St. Nicholas came with a bound.
He was dressed all in fur, from his head to his foot,
And his clothes were all tarnished with ashes and
soot; A bundle of toys he had flung on his back,

And he looked like a peddler just opening his pack.
His eyes -- how they twinkled! his dimples how merry!
His cheeks were like roses, his nose like a cherry!
His droll little mouth was drawn up like a bow,
And the beard of his chin was as white as the snow;

The stump of a pipe he held tight in his teeth,
And the smoke it encircled his head like a wreath;
He had a broad face and a little round belly,
That shook, when he laughed like a bowlful of jelly
He was chubby and plump, a right jolly old elf,

And I laughed when I saw him, in spite of myself;
A wink of his eye and a twist of his head,
Soon gave me to know I had nothing to dread;
He spoke not a word, but went straight to his work,
And filled all the stockings; then turned with a jerk,

And laying his finger aside of his nose,
and giving a nod, up the chimney he rose;
He sprang to his sleigh, to his team gave a whistle,
And away they all flew like the down of a thistle.
But I heard him exclaim, ere he drove out of sight,
"Happy Christmas to all, and to all a good night"

(Moore, 1823)

During the Christmas season, our house was beautifully decorated with *flycatchers* which were made from colored sheets of tissue paper. The paper was folded in a specific manner and cut in *origami–like* fashion. The catcher was unfolded and shaken to make a long, attractive hanging for the ceiling.

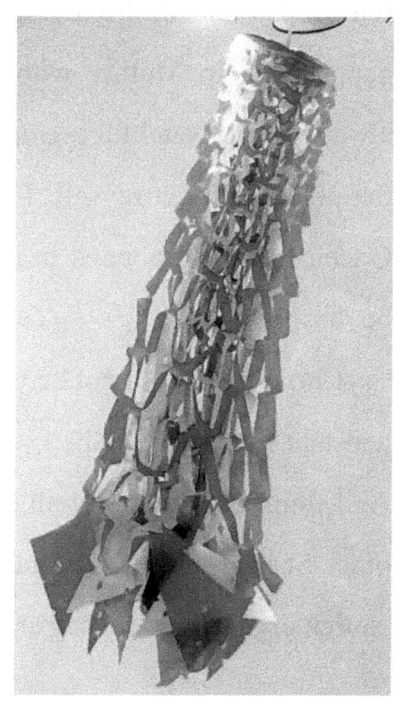

Courtesy Wendell Stevens

On the table was a vase of flowers which Mother created using crepe paper. She skillfully cut out petals and leaves which she curled and shaped with her scissors to form some of the most beautiful flowers; then she attached them to wire stems that she completely covered with the green crepe paper. There were new curtains at the windows and pretty runners or doilies on the tables, all made by our highly creative Mother.

The front room of the house was made spic and span. Drawers were emptied of all *curuttle*. Furniture was polished and the crystal and other pieces in the china cabinet were removed, washed, dried and put back into place. I was very happy to help Mother with this on several occasions. She always kept a watchful eye on me so that I did not break any of the pieces and cut myself. Everything was sparkling clean. If Queen Elizabeth popped in for a surprise visit, she would not be disappointed!

Christmas would not be Christmas without Nennie, another constant in our lives. She lived a few minutes from our house. As I think of it now, we all seemed to live very close to each other. She was one of my Tata's many sisters, my godmother and church organist for as long as I can remember.

Cousin Yvonne and Nennie

She patiently trained our choir and rehearsed with us all the songs we needed to know for our Christmas and Easter programs. She led our Sunday services with the melodious notes of the organ which she played so skillfully for so many years until her untimely passing.

> *"Christmas is a season not only for rejoicing but of reflection."*
>
> Winston Churchill

~Playing House~

"Play is the work of a child;
It is not a trivial pursuit."

Alfred Adler

This was a fun time for us children when we impersonated the adults and played *shop* which was where we pretended to sell groceries. We wanted to be grownup and it seemed like such a long time before that would happen.

Sometimes we played at Mamina's house and sometimes we played at our house under the big *tommon* tree. Oona, our cousin who was *Taunts* Ivy's daughter played with us and of course, she always brought *Goldilocks,* her *dolly* who was dressed in red. Goldilocks went everywhere that Oona went. Eldie also came to play with us.

Source: my cousin, Andrew St. Hilaire – Oona with Goldilocks, Me, Maizie and Keith

We took turns playing the role of shopkeeper and were quite imaginative when it came to deciding what represented certain kinds of food. We scooped up mounds of dirt from around the yard and sold it as *brown sugar*. We used Mother's scissors to cut the leaves of the lilies into tiny strips and they became chibble or scallions.

The bulbs at the roots of the lily plants were re-named *onions*, and the wild, parasitic yellow love plant became *macaroni* after we broke it in little pieces. If we had known about spaghetti, I suppose we could have given it that name instead.

We pretended to be grown up and padded our blouses with paper to simulate breasts. We took turns playing the role of the pregnant mother by stuffing wads of paper into our underwear so that we would have a round belly. We played with our dolls and treated them like newborn babies, feeding and changing their clothes. We gently held our dolls up to our "breasts" and pretended that we were breastfeeding them. We enjoyed our paper dolls as well, with the cut-out clothes which were secured to the dolls with tabs on various parts of the clothes.

Yellow Love Plant

Another playtime activity that we enjoyed was playing with the rag dolls that Mother made and stuffed. She embroidered facial features on the dolls. We derived many hours of happiness from this pastime of playing shop and pretending that we were adults.

> *"Play is often talked about as if it were a relief from serious learning, but for children play is serious learning. Play is really the work of childhood."*
>
> Fred Rogers

~My Tata – A Privileged Man~

"My father didn't tell me how to live.
He lived and let me watch him do it."

Clarence Budington Kelland

February 20th is the anniversary of Tata's death. It was a death that happened all too soon, and its suddenness was intensely overwhelming, leaving a gaping hole where my heart should be. We still had far-away places we wanted to travel to, and I had perhaps one more *hospital story* to share with him. As I write this chapter about him, my mind is flooded with a host of wonderful memories.

He was the son of Eloise and Harold Flax whom we called Grandfather. He lived very close to where we were. Tata was a dashing young man when he married our Mother and was one

My dear, dear Tata (deceased)

of the hardest working men I have ever known. He was tireless in his efforts to provide the best for his family. Toward that end, he did whatever was necessary to earn a meager salary in those days of our childhood. He was a carpenter by trade, and I told him once that he was just like Jesus. He answered that he was a sinner and Jesus was not.

I spent many happy afternoons with him under the *tommon* tree watching him *plane* wood and measure and cut the appropriate pieces for his building project. In the process, I got an education in tools and how to use them. He was so patient in teaching me and answering my many questions.

He also worked on the island of St. John for a while for the appalling pay of twenty-nine dollars a week! He did not complain because working away from home sometimes was necessary for him to take care of his children. He always said, *"whatever I do, I do for my children."* He worked hard and diligently so that we could go abroad to attend school and achieve the higher education he was not privileged to have. Although his earnings seemed meager when compared to the salaries of today, he and Mother saved what they could and together they accomplished their goals.

Tata told me in later years when he visited me that he credited Mother with being frugal so that they could realize their dreams. He said if he had to do it over, he would marry her again. It has been said that the best thing a man can do for his children is to love their Mother. I am confident that he showed how much we meant to him – he loved our Mother.

In addition to his beautiful carpentry work Tata was also a government employee, working in various capacities. It was a post his grandfather also held for many years before him. He served as the *Local constable* who is the equivalent of a police officer. He carried a *stick* and a flashlight but no firearm. His presence at community functions was enough to keep everyone on their best behaviour.

He was the *Registrar* of births and deaths on the island, so whenever a child was born or a death occurred, those events were registered at our house by the surviving relatives. A small room at our house was designated as the office where Tata conducted all his government business.

Tata was also the *tax collector* and everyone who owned anything of any value dutifully trekked to our house to pay taxes for their houses, dogs, horses and boats. I was about eight years old when he taught me how to write a receipt for the taxes that were paid. He was also the *postman* (I thought that he, like Mother, could do everything!), so all of the mail for the island's inhabitants was sent to our house from Tortola in big brown burlap sacks – the same ones that played the role of *stockings* at Christmas.

As a result of the multiple hats that Tata wore, he was almost always one of the first people that visitors to the island encountered. Tata loved meeting new people and welcomed everyone with open arms to Virgin Gorda. Consequently, many lasting friendships were formed over the years – something Tata delighted in.

In later years, a government building was erected on Virgin Gorda, giving recognition to the Flaxes for their civic contributions over the years.

The Flax Building

Tata was very much a "people" person - a very social person, who loved Virgin Gorda in a way that no one else did. He lovingly called it *The Rock.* Many years later, it would be said of him, "Virgin Gorda was Malvin, and Malvin was Virgin Gorda." His pride in being a Virgin Gordian was evident to anyone who knew him. While he enjoyed his many travels throughout the world in later years he always wanted to go back home to The Rock. He encouraged visitors to return to the island and in doing so he cultivated friends in countries near and far. I think he was the perfect Tourism Ambassador long before anyone even thought of tourism as an industry!

Tata was very even-tempered and good natured. He would absent himself from the situation instead of becoming embroiled in an argument. Even as a child I never heard Tata argue with Mother. If Mother fussed or argued with him about anything, he would take a walk or he would say to her, *"when you're tired, you will stop."* He was peace-loving and cherished harmonious surroundings.

Tata was a talker. Mother called him a *long meter* which is a term used to describe a person who likes to talk for long periods. Tata fit the bill perfectly. He stopped to chat with young and old alike, about any subject. If he were delayed getting home, it usually was because he met someone he stopped to talk with. He had an inquisitive mind and wanted to learn new things, so he always asked questions. I sometimes wonder what his occupation would have been if he had been given the opportunity to go to school in New York as he wanted to do many years earlier. He was fascinated with languages and if he met someone who spoke Spanish, there was no hesitation on his part to show off the few Spanish phrases that he knew.

He was actively involved in various activities in his church. He was a choir member with a rich baritone voice of operatic quality that could not be missed. He took his role of a licensed Lay Leader seriously and simply served in any capacity in which he was needed. He was a vestryman which meant that he was a member of the leading body that saw to the church's activities.

He also held the titles of Sunday School Superintendent as well as Cemetery Superintendent for the graveyard at the church. He attended services every Sunday and in between, regardless of sunshine or rain. He was a devout Christian who believed strongly in *the man up there*. On special occasions, such as Methodist Harvest, Tata joined Mother at her church for their much-anticipated duet. He said on many occasions that we served one God, so it did not matter what church we attended.

Tata was actively involved in the community, always making time to help others. One of the most interesting things I remember him doing was notarizing documents. As people brought their papers to him, he spread a red, heated substance on the paper and then pressed his embosser into it while it was soft, leaving the imprint of the tool on the document. He then signed it, making the document an official one, with its bright red seal.

One of the things that Tata was very proud of was becoming a member of the Most Excellent Order of the British Empire (MBE). This designation is awarded by Queen Elizabeth twice during the year, usually on New Year's Day and on her official birthday in June. It is bestowed on civilians in recognition of meritorious service.

Tata was tireless in his efforts to help the people of our island in any capacity. When cars came to the island, Tata bought a truck and he never hesitated to give someone a ride even though it might mean going completely out of his way, in a totally different direction.

In the same manner, he frequently loaned out various carpentry tools or simply offered them to anyone who needed them. Needless to say, most of those tools were never seen again. Tata's attitude was that he would just buy another of whatever it was.

He was the Captain of the Boys Brigade and took great pride in his leadership role. I recall seeing him with his group on one occasion when he explained and then demonstrated, the importance of good posture to them. He was a well-respected

Tata with his Boys' Brigade (front row, left)

man. Even his siblings did not call him Malvin, but instead they said "brother Malvin."

He was also an active member of the Lions Club service organization and this was an affiliation of which he was very proud. He wore the Lions pin everywhere he went and traveled extensively to attend the annual conventions. His affiliation and work with this organization earned him and Mother its highest honor – the Melvin Jones Fellow Award, which is acknowledgement of an individual's dedication to outstanding humanitarian service.

Both of my parents served tirelessly in this organization and gave of their time, talent and money, as needed.

Melvin Jones Fellow Award

Tata's favourite pastime was eating. In fact, he often said that people took a big chance sleeping all night without having any food to eat! He was very adventurous as far as food was concerned and he was always willing to sample new or different foods. His voracious appetite was evidenced by his empty plate every time he had a meal. We often joked with him that we did not need to wash his plate!

Regardless of how much he ate, he always had room for dessert. If you asked him whether or not he wanted dessert, he did a special little toss of his head to the side, as if to say, "How can you even ask me that – of course I want dessert!" Yes, he had the proverbial sweet tooth. He loved ice cream so when he visited me in later years, I always made sure that I had on hand several containers of different flavours for his pleasure and sheer enjoyment.

He lovingly tended to our assortment of animals – cows, goat and sheep which at some point in their lives provided food for us. It was hard work, moving the animals from one pasture to another so that they would have food, especially when the weather was dry, but Tata never complained. He milked the cows every morning so that we always had a supply of fresh milk...... and he continued to plant more fruit trees, usually consulting the reliable old Farmer's Almanac for a good planting day.

He loved to work in his garden, and it was something he did on a daily basis. In fact, that is precisely where he was when he was suddenly taken from us. He always had time to plant another fruit tree or look for seeds that he could plant to see if they would *germinate.* He loved that word! When he visited me in California years later, he was careful to save the seeds of any fruit that was different from those in the Virgin Islands.

Indeed, our property was surrounded with mango, banana, soursop, sugar apple, mesple, pineapple and sea grape trees. He was tireless in his efforts to provide fruit for his children when they came home to visit.

Soursop

A favourite memory is that when Tata went to Road Town, Tortola for government business, he never failed to return without a treat for us. He remembered to stop at Mrs. Douglas' shop, The Cool Corner, to purchase some patties which were little fried turnovers filled with meat, in a half-moon shape. They were tasty and we always wanted more, but we also heeded Mother's advice to share everything we had with each other.

He also sometimes bought avocados which we called *pears*. In addition, he never forgot to stop somewhere for candy to satisfy his "sweet tooth."

Sugar Apple

Another fruit that we all enjoyed was the sugar apple, a three-dimensional fruit, green on the outside with deliciously sweet, white pulp and small black seeds on the inside. This fruit could also be boiled before it could ripen and become soft and was sometimes eaten as an accompaniment to boiled fish.

Uncle Hartman (deceased)

Tata *set fish pots* with grandfather (his father), and Uncle Hartman (his brother), at Taylor's Bay so that fresh fish was another delicacy we could enjoy. Tata also learned to spear fish and often accompanied his German friend, Mr. Kolby, on a fishing excursion. Mr. Kolby owned a refrigerator and since we did not enjoy that luxury, all the fish were kept at his house and retrieved when Mother wanted to prepare fish for our lunch.

If you wanted anything packaged securely for shipping, just give it to Tata! It was fascinating to sit and watch him securing a box with tape. You wondered how anyone would ever get into it and if at some point they would simply give up. Yes, he always did a masterful taping job!

In 1964 just after I had gone abroad to further my education, Laurence Rockefeller, an entrepreneur and a philanthropist from the United States brought progress and prosperity to the island in the form of an upscale resort which he named Little Dix Bay Resort. Tata worked as the foreman overseeing the workers who cleared the heavy vegetation to make way for the first paved roads this island would have.

In his later years, Tata loved to travel, and he did, extensively. He saw more of the United States that I have, although I live here. He was "privileged" to visit Buckingham Palace and the Houses of Parliament in London, he climbed the Spanish Steps in Rome, Italy, he watched the flamenco dancers in Spain, he made snowballs in Switzerland and he fulfilled his childhood dream of going to Gibraltar where he had up-close views of the Barbary apes. His goal was to visit all the continents, and he almost did; he had just one more

Tata as foreman, on the right

to go. He never assumed that he would be here tomorrow, so he took nothing for granted; he considered every experience in his life "a privilege."

> *"Remembering you is easy – I do it every day;*
> *Missing you is the heartache that never goes away."*
>
> Author unknown

~Declining Customs~

*"It takes an endless amount of
history to make even a little tradition."*

Henry James

My father, grandfather, uncle and other neighbourhood people went out and *set fish pots* which were specially made square boxes of chicken wire with a trap door to catch the fish which were usually shared with friends and neighbours. There was no lack of fresh seafood, including giant lobsters, one of which could feed a family.

Many people are unaware that the cashew grows on the end of a fruit we called a cherry. The pulp of that fruit was usually stewed with sugar and spices and eaten as a dessert. It was a delicacy we referred to as "stew cherry." The nut of this fruit was roasted on a metal circle that had been cut from a drum or some other large aluminum container. It was placed on three large stones out in the open or on a coal pot, and a fire was built underneath. The nuts were tossed about slowly until they became roasted cashews, although we called them *cherry nuts*.

On my visits home in later years, my aunt, Taunie sometimes surprised me with some of them.

Cashew

A common practice in many families was administering daily doses of cod liver oil to their children. I remember the routine so well: Mother measured out a teaspoon of the oily liquid, we opened our mouths, pinched our noses and swallowed, hating the disgusting, fishy taste which we again tasted if we belched (burped) during the day. In addition, there was also a regular dosing of castor oil to *clean out our insides!*

Some adults, including Tata, also drank shark oil which was made from the liver and fat of the shark. This oil was supposed to be highly effective against colds and other diseases. Just as there was a bush remedy for everything, there was one to be used in the event we ate something that gave us a *pudging*.

My observation is that Old Year's Night, now called New Year's Eve, is also quite different from the days of my childhood. We went to "Watch Night Service" at eleven thirty in the evening and sang and prayed about whatever the New Year would bring.

It is now a time that is filled with merriment and celebrations in stark contrast to the days of long ago when it was regarded as a solemn occasion. Solemn, because it was unknown what misfortune the New Year would bring to each family. It was also a common practice for people to pay any existing bills on that day so that they would begin the New Year debt-free. There were no banks, checks or credit cards. It was strictly a cash society.

Another time of joy was the picking of the genip, a small round fruit which has a slightly sweet/tart flavor and grows in bunches, like the way that grapes grow. Our neighbour, Miss Ethel, who lived just to the west of us had a monstrous tree on her property and every year, on a designated date, several young men climbed the tree and dropped bunches of genips to the eager, waiting hands below. This was a much – anticipated event and there were always enough genips for everyone to garner a good supply.

On visits home now I observe that some people will simply walk onto your property and pick the genips or any other fruit without even asking permission. Sadly, some things are just not what they used to be.

Genips

The coal pit was another amazing accomplishment of the men on our island. The process for obtaining the charcoal for the coal pot was a fascinating thing to watch. The men got together and dug a gigantic, shallow hole in the ground which was known as a *coal-pit*. A large number of tree branches which had been stripped of their leaves were layered on *runners* in the pit. The runners allowed the fire to get underneath the wood and burn all of it.

Coal pit - Source: BVI Welcome

When the wood was built up to the desired level, tree branches were placed on the sides and the top. It was then covered entirely with dirt, leaving an opening in the side of the mound so that they could light the wood inside. As the wood burned plumes of smoke emanated from this hole. The pit was left alone for a while - several days or a week. As the wood turned into charcoal, the height of the pit dropped down and soon there were no smoke emissions, an indication that inside was rich, black charcoal, ready for a waiting coal-pot.

Another practice was watching quietly as sea turtles came up on the sand to lay and bury their eggs which were not allowed to hatch but instead were quickly gathered up by waiting hands. The men of the island knew when this event would occur, so everyone gathered and stayed out of sight.

It was a nighttime activity observed and enjoyed by many. The eggs were perhaps a little larger than a golf ball and were simply boiled and eaten. At one time the meat of the green turtle and hawksbill turtle was used for food on a regular basis. Yes, turtle stew and turtle soup were both quite enjoyable!

I am glad to see that Guy Fawkes' day is still celebrated (usually on the field west of the Methodist Church). It was celebrated with a huge bonfire - an event we all looked forward to as children. This is a holiday which began as a celebration to acknowledge the survival of King James after an attempt on his life in the House of Lords in England in 1605 and continues to this day.

An activity that many of us looked forward to every year was decorating the church for Palm Sunday services. On Saturday afternoon the floor was swept, and the windowsills were dusted followed by the adornment of the windows and doors which were outlined with palm branches. Some branches were also placed at the altar area. The placement of the palm branches represents the triumphal entry of Jesus into Jerusalem during the final days before the Last Supper.

On Sunday everyone wore something green to church services.

"Growth and fulfillment come from abandoning old practices and embracing new ones."

Brian Tracy

~Mamina – Our Loving Family Matriarch~

"You don't really understand something unless you can explain it to your grandmother."

Albert Einstein

Eloise was my paternal grandmother; we lovingly called her Mamina. I am not sure how we arrived at that name, but my guess is that the first grandchild was unable to fully pronounce the word "grandma" or "grandmother" so "Mamina" stuck and those of us who came after followed suit. Mamina was one of the kindest people I ever knew. As I think of her, I realize that we did a lot of things together.

When Tata traveled to Road Town, Tortola to take care of government business, it was Mamina who took the long trek to the pasture to milk the cows. Like Tata, she showed us how to

My dear Mamina (deceased)

pull on the cow's tits to squeeze out the milk and of course she always allowed us a sample of that warm liquid. For us it was a daily walk to the south, on the road to the Baths, to take care of the cows……. and we still managed to get to school on time. That is probably because we seemed to get up with the chickens!

Mamina owned her own flock of goats and sheep which were pastured at the Country or at Red Point. Day after day she lovingly tended them, moving them from one area to another for food. Just getting to her animals was a challenge as the roads were nothing more than narrow, rugged paths with outcropping of rocks along the way, making her journey a very treacherous one. When it rained the water simply gushed along those roads and took anything in its path including Taunie (my aunt Lillian) who once lost her footing and became a victim of the muddy torrent. Luckily, she was able to grab a fallen tree branch, preventing serious bodily injury but suffering severe scrapes and bruises.

Mamina spent most of her day caring for the animals and it was evening time before she returned to her home. She usually stopped at our house for a while and had "tea" which was just a snack. Sometimes she spent hours there telling *"ole time"* stories as she called them. As children we were always fascinated by some of the tales about people who had died many years before.

Mamina was a devout Christian and attended church services every Sunday at the Anglican Church. She was always intent on doing *"the Master's will."* She always looked as if she just stepped out of a fashion magazine, decked out in her finest clothes, including hat and gloves. Her colors were well coordinated, and she was never without her jewelry. My sister and I remember her fastidious dressing fondly and we often say that we got our sense of fashion from her. She usually had lunch with us after church service and we frequently reminded her that the doctor said she should not use salt because of her high blood pressure. Her reply: "What does he know?" as she sprinkled more salt on her food. She had a mind of her own and no one was going to change it!

Her generosity was legendary whether it was with her time or something tangible. Although she suffered with arthritis she was always "trying her best" and never too tired to do anything that was asked of her.

Occasionally she received a large box of *"ready-made"* clothes from her sister-in-law who lived in New York. Instead of keeping these beautiful designer clothes for herself she shared them with family members. She set a date and time for the grand opening of the box and all the female members of her immediate family were allowed to select whatever they liked best. This was Mamina's style!

She loved her grandchildren and never used a harsh word with any of us. She had the softest hair which she conditioned with coconut oil and styled with beautiful tortoise-shell combs and pins. Even after her hair had become almost white, the back of her head at the neck area was as black as ebony. She allowed us to comb her hair from time to time and as young girls we got great pleasure from creating all sorts of styles.

Speaking of hair, Mamina was a little eccentric in a habit she cultivated over the years. After combing her hair, she carefully removed all stray hair from her comb and brush and stored the hair in shoeboxes. Over time she had collected quite a few of these. She made us all laugh as she told us that if she discarded her hair, she would become *"scatterbrained!"*

She was famous in our family for the "bush" tea she made from rock balsam and other bushes. When we were sick with colds or upset stomachs, nothing was more effective than Mamina's bush tea and other concoctions......and who could forget the poultices which were made from pieces of flannel cloth that had been coated with camphorated oil and other ingredients? These were placed on our chests when we had severe colds and coughs. Miraculously, in a day or so we were as good as new. As the years went by, there were fewer poultices being used and our chests and backs were instead rubbed by Mother with Vicks Vaporub which seemed to be highly effective. I still rub my chest with Vicks when I have a cold, wishing that Mother was the one doing the rubbing.

Home-made remedies were common treatments for whatever ailed us. There was no source of medical help on the island other than Miss Iris, the midwife who delivered all the babies, so self-help was the order of the day. Simple cuts and bruises were treated with the healing drops of the yellow liquid from the succulent leaves of the aloe vera plant which we knew as Simpi-vivy. Our Mamina swore by this treatment. We sometimes used it instead of soap for washing our hair as shampoo was not available to us. As Mother often said, necessity was the Mother of invention, so we improvised when we needed to do so.

Aloe Vera (Simpi-vivy)

We loved when Mamina treated us with her very tasty stuffed onions. She boiled whole onions and then separated the layers which she filled with a concoction of corned beef, potatoes and spices. After replacing the layers to form a ball, she rolled it in flour and then deep fried it in hot melted lard. It was a delicacy we all enjoyed, much as we did her stewed cherries which. as noted before were actually the fruit that grew at the end of the cashew nut.

She taught us to play the Chinese game of skill, known as Mahjong, which was played by four players with wooden tiles. We enjoyed playing this game with her, but try as we may, it seemed that she was always the winner –she never allowed us to win because as she said, that would not be learning the skill of the game.

Playing mahjong with Mamina was much like playing Chinese Checkers with Mother! They both very quietly contemplated their maneuvers and then skillfully executed them, much to the chagrin of all the other players who sometimes did not realize that the game was over!

Mamina and I wrote to each other from time to time and each time I visited her at home she always said I would not get any more letters because she would soon be gone. Much to our joy, she lived many years past her predictions, and we were able to write to each other more than she thought we would.

A letter from Mamina

*"We are the keepers of the memories;
a sacred trust given by one who has journeyed on."*
Glenda Stansbury

~Special Memories of My Siblings and Me~

*"Siblings will take different paths and
Life may separate them…but they will
Forever be bonded by having begun
Their journey in the same boat."*

Author unknown

My memories of growing up with my siblings are not many as they were all young when I went away to school, but there are a few that have stayed with me.

Keith:

Even as a little boy, my older brother, Keith, had the best sense of humour. Mother used to say that he was always *grinning* because he was very often laughing about something. He was also a very sound sleeper. It was customary to leave doors open and this was sometimes an invitation for chickens to take a stroll inside.

One morning as a hen made her way into the bedroom where Keith was sleeping, I attempted to chase her out, but my actions caused her to run and jump on the bed where Keith was sound asleep. She stepped along the full length of his body and ran across his face. Keith slept through the entire episode!

Maizie:

My only sister, Maizie, was a sickly child and as a result she missed some of our playtimes. When she was a little girl, she suffered with severe asthma attacks which occurred quite frequently and our parents attempted every remedy they knew of, or were told about, to make her well. This included a generous helping of fresh turtle blood. Ugh!! I remember that Mother and Tata made every effort to get Tedral, allegedly an asthma medication, from Puerto Rico. It was a pale yellow, creamy liquid which seemed to help Maizie during her asthmatic episodes.

At one point, Tata even cut down several of the blooming plants on the property when it was suggested that the pollen was the cause of her asthma. I was always secretly afraid that she was going to die as my other siblings did, but fortunately, she outgrew this illness at an early age and was able to join in our play activities.

Ellsworth:

This memory of my younger brother, Ellsworth, affectionately called Boy Blue was not a particularly good one, but certainly my book would not be complete without its inclusion. He was about five years old when he followed me to a table outside one evening to watch me light the Coleman lantern. I could do this expertly, having done it many times before. It was dusk outside.

The process involved using the generating can to pour alcohol into the designated cup and scraping a match to light it. My brother was quite small, and his head and neck area just barely reached the tabletop which he leaned against. Unknown to us some of the alcohol which had overflowed also touched his skin. Suddenly my dear little brother was on fire around the head and neck area. I quickly grabbed my skirt and wrapped around him and realized that my arm was also on fire!

Mother and Tata came running when our sister, Maizie screamed that Boy Blue was on fire. Tata took him to Miss Iris, the nurse on the island, to be treated. I remember being very frightened because I thought that my brother would also die. Thankfully, he did not.

Me:

It seemed that Mother and Tata were always buying shoes for me. For some unexplained reason, my shoes became worn more quickly than those of my brothers and sister. I had to listen to them complain about the fact that I was getting new shoes all the time. However, in the process, I also gained the unflattering title of "iron foot."

I was also the most serious of my siblings (as evidenced in some photographs), and I was affectionately nicknamed Chunkie (pronounced Choonkie) at birth by my Tata when he first saw me.

Here I am with my very serious face wearing my very patriotic dress.

Me (about 10 years old)

In the picture below I am wearing one of my favourite dresses with my hair in braids. I am again the picture of seriousness.

Me, second from the right (as a teenager)

Perhaps my serious demeanor and my membership in the St. John's Ambulance Brigade served as a precursor to my nursing career which was to come later in life. The St. John Ambulance Brigade is the place where I learned basic first aid principles and the meaning of such words as "apoplexy" which refers to bleeding in the internal organs. However, at that time it was the common name for a stroke.

I remember that when May May's husband, Mr. Howard died suddenly and neighbours gathered, there was talk about him having had a stroke. I was proud that I knew the fancy name of apoplexy. When I told Mother and Tata that Mr. Howard had apoplexy Tata said proudly, "you can be a doctor!"

As members of the St. John Ambulance Brigade, we dressed in white uniforms with white socks and white scarves around our heads. We looked very much like a group of nuns. During our instruction we learned that the Brigade had been established in the 1800's after World War ll to provide first aid and care for injured survivors.

Me – the shortest one in the group

We attended meetings on a regular basis and were taught how to clean minor wounds and apply the dreaded antiseptic mercurochrome, which not only burned intensely, but turned one's skin orange red. We learned the correct way to wrap different types of bandages properly and securely. We also learned to apply splints in the event of a broken bone and to apply pressure above the site of an injury in order to prevent excessive bleeding.

> *"Sibling relationships outlast marriages,*
> *survive the death of parents, resurface after quarrels*
> *that would sink any friendship.*
> *They flourish in a thousand*
> *incarnations of*
> *closeness and distance,*
> *warmth, loyalty and distrust."*
>
> Erica Goode

~Mother-isms~

"No one in life will ever love you the way your mother does. There is no love as pure, as unconditional and strong as a Mother's love….
And I will never be loved that way again."

Hope Edelman

This book would be incomplete if I did not include some of Mother's favourite quotes, which in retrospect, were bits of sage advice on many subjects. She always seemed to have the appropriate answer for any situation.

Work:

-Things done by halves are never done right

-If you start it, you must finish it

-Hard work never killed anyone

-Hard work builds character

-If it's worth having, it's worth working hard for

Hope:

-As long as there is life, there is hope

-You must live in hope even if you die in despair

Contentment:

-Do not want what anyone else has

-Be content with what God has given you

-Do not focus on money – it is the root of all evil

Sharing/Saving:

-Even if it's just a fly wing, you must share it

Always try to save a little even it is only five cents – it will add up

Prayer:

-Believe in God

-Always pray about everything

-Remember to say your prayers

-God may take seven years to answer your prayer but he will

Life:

-If you can't do better, say "no matter."

-Necessity is the Mother of invention.

Avoiding Nosiness:

-I only know what you tell me.

Obedience:

-The ship that is not ruled by the rudder, the rocks will pick her up

Conservation

-Waste not, want not

-Don't be too quick to throw things away

Determination:

-If at first you don't succeed, try, try again.

-Practice makes perfect

-Perseverance is the Mother of success

In retrospect, we did not realize it then.......we were too young to fully understand......but ultimately, these "isms" were great lessons that shaped our lives…..taught to us by a very wise woman whom everyone referred to as Miss Eda or Mrs. Flax….. but to us she was simply Mother.

My dear, dear Mother (deceased)

*"Sometimes the strength of motherhood
Is greater than natural laws"*

Barbara Kingsolver

~In Memoriam – My Siblings Lost~

> *"You think you have time."*
> Buddha

As a child I had no knowledge of the significance of a child's death for a parent. I could not begin to comprehend the devastating sense of loss they endured. I only knew that when death occurred that person was no longer there, and sadness and grief seemed to overwhelm everyone. It was a time of frequent, overflowing tears and black clothes which were worn for several months with a gradual transition to black and white, and eventually grey, as was the custom of that time. This period of mourning usually lasted for one year.

The absence of technology and the lack of a morgue or a process to preserve the dead meant that funerals happened very quickly and efficiently. As soon as death occurred the inhabitants of the island were notified by the tolling of the church bell and the gravediggers promptly began the task of preparing the plot for burial the following day. The coffin was crafted of pine wood and covered with an embossed fabric (commonly referred to as funeral cloth) in deep purple or dark gray color reserved for just this purpose. It was subsequently decorated with silver or gold-colored hardware. Some of the island's inhabitants pre-purchased these materials and kept them under their beds for the appropriate time. The deceased remained in the home with a folded handkerchief placed under the chin and tied on the top of the head and the face was covered.

A "wake" was held in the home of the deceased on the evening of the same day and was a very solemn occasion with singing of mournful hymns and prayers. There was no lack of tears or nose-blowing – it was a time of raw emotion. There was no eating or drinking. Until late in 1963 there were no automobiles on the island, so funeral processions were long, mournful walks as everyone trudged along on foot on the uneven, rocky, dirt roads until arrival at the designated place of burial. It was an unpleasant experience with the blazing hot sun overhead and the dust swirling in the air as the arid earth was disturbed by the individual foot traffic on this sad journey.

My little sister, Dahlia, was the first of my siblings to leave us one month after Christmas on January 24, 1950. She succumbed to a severe respiratory infection which was said to be pneumonia. She was thirteen months old and I was a little over four years old, but I still remember the little white chiffon dress with puffed sleeves that Mother made for her. Imagine sewing a dress in which your child, your baby, will be buried! Imagine building a little coffin in which you will bury your child. I cannot comprehend the heart-rending pain and sorrow that Mother and Tata must have felt, yet they persevered.

Keithley joined Dahlia in September of 1952 at the age of one month. He had been born with the congenital anomaly of cleft palate and harelip which presented a major feeding challenge as the milk leaked out and around his mouth, making quite a mess. I remember how gently Mother cleaned his little face.

Mother traveled alone with Keithley to Puerto Rico where he was scheduled for three surgeries to correct the deformity. As a young girl I heard the adults discussing the fact that he developed an infection after the second procedure and died. He was buried in Puerto Rico and Mother returned home alone – empty-handed.

She described his little casket in great detail, graphically detailing the white angels on the blue background of his coffin. I remember her telling the story with a constant flow of tears running down her face. Now that I am older, I cannot imagine her going through that experience alone. It seemed that she cried for a long time after that……and then there was Ken. He was four and a half years old when our family was devastated yet again. He and Tata were inseparable companions - you truly never saw one without the other and I remember him so vividly.

Ken did not feel well for a couple of days and did not appear to be getting better, so Tata took him to Road Town to the doctor on the "Petrel," one of the local sailboats that was scheduled to continue to St. Thomas.

Mother had noticed a couple of *"omens"* which foretold death, according to the superstitions of our culture. The blowing of the Queen conch shell was a means of nautical communication in the islands, so when she heard the familiar sound signaling the return of the "Petrel" to Virgin Gorda, she started to cry. She told me that something was wrong. Just as she predicted, Tata soon arrived with Ken's little, lifeless body wrapped and lying on a pediatric stretcher. It was the fifth of January, 1955 and Ken had been claimed by bronchitis.

Who dies of bronchitis? Unfortunately, we were living at a time when antibiotics had not yet been developed and the prognosis for the most minor conditions was frequently grave. The fact that there was no medical facility on the island did not help matters.

So, once more, there was another little outfit to be made, another grave to be dug and yet another little coffin to be constructed. I remember the long walk from our church, trudging once again in single file down that all too familiar uneven dirt road to the Flax graveyard where Ken was laid to rest beside our sister, Dahlia. I can see in my mind's eye the waves of stifling dust in the air from each step that took Ken to his final resting place.

I cannot ever forget how Tata cried. It was the most profound, almost howling sound I have ever heard, and which seemed to come from deep within his soul. Sometimes I think that I can close my eyes and still hear him, sounding as if he himself were dying.

For many months while Mother sobbed quietly, Tata had frequent bouts of mournful crying. He sat on a chair in the front yard and stared into space for hours at a time. Mother frequently had to encourage him to eat. He seemed completely dejected and almost destroyed by the loss of Ken. He did not speak to anyone. He appeared to go about his life in a robotic fashion, and lost interest in any community activities other than church services on Sunday. He and Mother both grieved in their own way and after some time had passed, life appeared to return to normal.

"The song is ended but the melody lingers on."-
Irving Berl

~*A Letter to My Beloved Parents*~

"The death of any loved parent is an incalculable lasting blow. Because no one ever loves you again like that."

Brenda Ueland

My dearest Mother and Tata,

You are both gone now, and my one regret is that you will never be able to read my book. I know you would be so proud of my effort. On the other hand, you may be hovering over my shoulder while I write because sometimes, I feel your presence. I can only hope that you are reading as I write.

You were both the most incredible parents any child could hope to have – always loving, nurturing.......always working hard to give us the privileges you did not enjoy in your younger years. You were determined that we should have a higher education and toward that end you allowed us all to go away to school.

You taught us by example to pray and to live decent lives, to be kind to others, to be respectful of not only our elders, but everyone we had contact with. You taught us to be grateful for all of God's blessings and not to be envious of other people's possessions.

You suffered in your individual ways through the unimaginable loss of three of your children, yet your faith and trust in the God you believed in did not waver. People of lesser faith would have crumbled, but you did not......you both soldiered on with strength from your Creator.

You instilled in us morals and values that continue to serve us well in our daily lives. You were a constant presence in our lives, although you did not pry or interfere. Mother, you always said, "I only know what you tell me."

Our family travels throughout Europe were special times with great memories not to be forgotten. Mother, you were so afraid to fly but you went anyway because Tata was the traveler who relished each new experience and was always eager to have the next one. He had traveled to all of the continents except Africa and when he stood on the sand in Costa del Sol, Spain and looked across the water towards Morocco, he said "now I can say that I have seen Africa!"

Tata, the sudden loss of you almost crushed me completely. I am so sorry that you died alone in your garden....you were such a "people" person, you should have been surrounded by lots of people...in retrospect, you were not alone – your God was there, and he noticed that you were very tired, so he gave you the rest you needed. There were days that I did not see how I could go on, but I have learned to accept that you are with me in spirit. The wonderful memories of you and all the things we did together have helped to soften the loss and I can finally smile again when I think of you now.

Mother, your chapter in this book is the longest one because there was so much to say about you. I am glad that I was able to spend the last five days of your life with you, to hold your hand, to sing to you, to tuck your blanket around you when you felt cold, to have you tell me that I was your "first-born" and to remind you of much I loved you, even on that last day when you no longer spoke.

I remember that day so well – you looked into my face so intensely as if you were seeing me for the first time, or as if it were the last time you would see me. I remember the times you wondered out loud why God was keeping you here and I reminded you of the Bible verse in the Book of John, Chapter 14, verse 2 where Jesus said *"In my father's house are many mansions....I go to prepare a place for you."* Your place became ready on May 31st.

The loss of you has been very difficult in a slightly different way, but I remind myself that you wanted to go, you were "ready" you said, you wanted to be with Tata and now you are.

It is a heartwarming experience to think of your parents and smile because your memories of them are such good and precious ones. You were both God-fearing people who lived according to the teachings of the Holy Bible which was front and center in our home.

It was a joy and privilege to care for both of you in my home when you were ill many years ago. I have spent my life caring for my patients who are literally strangers, and I was proud to show you the kind of nurse I am and how much I enjoy what I do. Tata, you were always very emotional when I took care of you because you did not want me to be a nurse in the first place, but you were incredibly grateful.

Being a daughter to the two of you has been the greatest honour and blessing of my life and my memories of you will always be greatly cherished and stored in the deep recesses of my heart.

The fact that you are both no longer here still seems like a dream sometimes, but I am learning to live with your absence. I am surrounded with many reminders of you on a daily basis – your picture in my bedroom, flowers along the roadside, soup on the stove, the bicycle shop or hardware store on the way to work, the New Moon; I feel your touch in a gentle breeze and I hear your voices when certain hymns are sung so you see, you will always be remembered.

I know that we will see each other again one day and oh, what a joyous reunion that will be! My love for you is cemented in the deep recesses of my heart for all time. Rest in the eternal peace reserved for God's good and faithful servants.

For everything you brought to my life, for all the lessons you taught me, for sharing in my sadness and my joys, for being wonderful grandparents to my children and for all the sacrifices you made along your life's journey, I say, "Thank you, thank you, my dearest Mother and Tata."

With my deepest love and with eternal gratitude,
Your "first-born,"
Chunkie

> "*The most important influence*
> *On a child is the character of its parents,*
> *rather than this or that single event.*" –
>
> Erich Fromm

~Epilogue~

"Time is the coin of your life. It is the only coin you have, and only you can determine how it will be spent. Be careful lest you let other people spend it for you."

Carl Sandburg

The Virgin Gorda I wrote about is far different today from the one on which I spent my formative years and resulted in a great deal of retrospective thinking as I recalled my early years. It is amazing how many memories the mind can catalog and how, after many years, they can be retrieved and relived.

The construction of the island's first luxury resort at Little Dix Bay in 1964 initiated a period of expansion and much-needed economic development which resulted in a major construction boon for the island. This resort built by Laurence Rockefeller, an American philanthropist, necessitated the concurrent development of the island's entire infrastructure since such basic services as indoor plumbing, electricity and paved roads were conspicuously absent.

The population today resembles a montage in which pieces have come together to create one beautiful unit. It is now comprised of the natives and those who migrated from different countries throughout the world and those who came from surrounding islands to seek employment at the resort and settled on Virgin Gorda permanently.

According to Maurer (1997), ordinances established in the late 1960s referred to "belonger" status in an attempt to restrict the actions of "persons not deemed to belong to the territory of the Virgin Islands" but who wished to enter and reside in the territory.

As one might logically conclude, immigrants married the natives, so while the original tapestry has changed, it has been transformed into one that is now woven with new threads of individual colours that are different but add their own brilliance to the vibrant colours of the new tapestry. The stranger whom I pass on the street now is frequently a relative I have not yet met, but there are still a few of the "oldies" who remember Virgin Gorda the way it used to be.

Speaking of oldies, we celebrated Mother's 100th birthday with a special Thanksgiving Service at her church where she was regaled with special musical and oral selections by family members, as well as the presentation of a card and flowers from Queen Elizabeth. Mother enjoyed lots of cake (her favourite thing to eat) at home afterwards. It seemed that most of Virgin Gorda wanted to be in the presence of this island's only centenarian, as there was standing room only at our house! It was a wonderful celebration – one which we will not soon forget.

Unfortunately, both of my parents are gone now but I am left with a multitude of loving memories. Tata was taken suddenly on February 20, 2003, and Mother was called away on May 31, 2019, six months and two days after her Centennial Celebration, halfway to one hundred and one! She slipped away silently in her sleep during the early morning hours to be with the Lord whom she loved and trusted all her life and to be reunited with Tata, the love of her life. She lived a good, long life in which she witnessed many of the changes on Virgin Gorda.

Today, Virgin Gorda no longer lacks paved roads, automobiles, electricity, indoor plumbing, supermarkets and little pricey boutiques designed to attract tourists. Progress has introduced the products and practices of the modern world to this once unspoiled island, but unfortunately adversity came along for the ride. It is a hallmark of progress – the good along with the bad.

A decline in cultural practices and moral values, a crime rate that was once non-existent, along with unsavoury attitudes and language are some of the negatives that have come with progress. However, the positives outweigh the negatives, so, I implore you to drop in for a visit – that is what my Tata would ask you to do, enjoy the beaches, the people, the smog-free air, enjoy your own pace on "island time."

While Virgin Gorda has metamorphosed from an undeveloped place of innocence and serenity into one with more worldly attributes and modern conveniences, its resilient people have survived the ravages of catastrophic weather events in recent years. The strength of these people can be seen and heard in conversations with them, in the rebuilding of their savagely destroyed properties and in their optimistic outlook toward the future.

Despite the unprecedented destruction from which it continues to valiantly recover, the island is still one of unsurpassed beauty, it is still "home" no matter where I live or to what distant land I travel, and it is still one of "Nature's little Secrets."

> *"The pessimist complains about the wind;*
> *the optimist expects it to change;*
> *the realist adjusts the sails."*
>
> William Arthur Ward

~Accolades for the Author~

"In this impressive debut, Shaw tells a coming-of-age story of love and heartbreak. A vivid tale set in the Caribbean that illustrates how the past influences the future and the lessons that come with it."

Lisa Bellemore-Burnette, PhD, Educator

"Life has to do with legacy. The legacy of the Flax Family to the beautiful island of Virgin Gorda is rich with stories of inspiration, motivation, and determination along with their committed and dedicated service for the betterment of humanity. Reading this insightful book by Hilde Shaw will motivate us to value service to others as the price to be paid for living."

Dr. Whitford A. Shaw, Retired Pastor and Chaplain

"Hilde has done a phenomenal job in capturing her youthful days. I found myself recalling to memory life as I once knew it on both Tortola and Peter Island as I savoured her account of growing up in the Valley, Virgin Gorda. We have embraced a myriad of changes that came about through the years; however, it is hard, if not impossible to forget the "good old days" when we lived simply, and when we all aimed to "do justice and to love kindness, and to walk humbly with our God." I admire the candour with which she has penned this delightful memoir, and how she so aptly brought to life what she experienced over six decades ago. Try as we may, we are unable to turn back the hands of time. Nevertheless, it is refreshing to know that we can always let our fingers do the walking and turn the pages of this book....and read and remember how it used to be in the beautiful, unspoiled Virgin Islands once upon a time."

Andria Flax, Author of "The Way We Were."

"Ms. Hildegarde Shaw became my friend and Nurse mentor in 1987. In rare quiet moments between patients, she shared her "Island Life" stories. Fully intrigued, I encouraged Hilde to write a book and here it is! In her debut book, Sharing a Fly Wing, she tells the beautiful, poignant details of her life as a young girl growing up on a remote island in the 1950's. This must-read, Island life tale is a breath of fresh air that transports one to a place of pure simplicity, far removed from the digital distraction and hurried pace of modern urban life."

Kelly Riley, Registered Nurse

"I am honoured to review Hilde Shaw's book about growing up on the island of Virgin Gorda in the British Virgin Islands. She gives a very personal account of her many memories and personal experiences that allow the reader to feel the special connections Hilde felt with her extraordinary parents and how those experiences continue to influence Hilde today. This book gives the reader a wonderful opportunity to experience the closeness of her growing up in a very special place with very special people."

Sue Fitch, Educator

"Hilde's detailed account of life in the islands during the days of her childhood captures the reader's interest and takes one along with her on the dirt roads and moonlight walks. The beauty and innocence of that time is sure to evoke nostalgia in those who knew her then."

Vanessa Noh, City Planner

"My friend has taken us on a journey into a time long past. One has only to close one's eyes and be transported back to the tranquility of this virgin, undeveloped island – the quiet of which was punctuated only by laughter of children or the call of animals. The story tells of bonds of love and trust, of morals and values, of joy and the pain of loss but still one senses the indomitable spirit of the people who lived there."

Jean Ryan, Attorney

"This wonderful memoir is filled with childhood memories of a time long ago when morals and values were cherished and nurtured. Hildegarde's attention to detail draws the reader in and one can imagine a place untouched by today's "noise" – a place almost "utopian" as she remembers it. She has painted a picture of innocence and happiness touched by periods of unimaginable pain for her family. In the end, she has created one beautiful tapestry of life on an undeveloped island."

Juanna Pinera, Registered Nurse

~Bibliography~

"The past is a place of reference, not a place of residence." –
Toby McKeehan

1. Cooper, Mary. 1744. Tommy Thumb's Song Book
2. "Copper Mine." n.d., p. 1. https://www.bvitourism.com/copper-mine.
3. Island Resources Foundation. 2012. An Environmental Profile of the Island of Virgin Gorda, British Virgin Islands
4. Garrett, Edward, Wolf, J. 1867. Aesop's Fables
5. Gellhorn, Martha. 2001. Travels with Myself and Another. Tarcher, New York.
6. Gilbert, Sir John, Tenniel, J., Harrison, W., Crane, W., McConnell, W., Zwecker, J. 1877.
7. Grafton, Richard. 1562. Abridgement of the Chronicles of England
8. Island Resources Foundation. 2012. An Environmental Profile of the Island of Virgin Gorda, British Virgin Islands

9. Ivimy, John. 1900. Complete version of Ye Three Blind Mice. F. Warne, London, New York
10. Kubler, Annie 2003. Row, Row, Row Your Boat. Child's Play International
11. Maurer, Bill. 1997. Re-charting the Caribbean: Land, Law, and Citizenship in the British Virgin Islands. The University of Michigan Press. Ann Arbor, MI
12. Mee, Arthur. 1908. Children's Encyclopedia
13. Moore, Clement Clarke, 1823. A Visit from Saint Nicholas
14. Mother Goose's Nursery Rhymes. George Routledge & Sons, London
15. O'Neal, Joseph R. 2004.Life Notes: Reflections of A British Virgin Islander. Xlibris Corporation.
16. Our History (2019) Retrieved from http://www.bvi.gov.vg/content/our-history.
17. Wadsworth, William. 1807. Poems. Longman, Hurst, Rees, & Orme, London
18. Virgin Islands 2010 Population and Housing Census Report. 2010
19. Warner, Anna Bartlett, 1860. Jesus Loves Me This I know.

"This above all: to thine own self be true"

Hamlet, William Shakespeare

~*About the Author*~

Hildegarde was born on Virgin Gorda in the British Virgin Islands and relocated as a teenager to New York to pursue her education. She is a Registered Nurse whose nursing career has been her life's passion.

She is mother to two children of her own and one stepson, grandmother to seven and great grandmother to three.

Hilde's other passion in which she frequently indulges is traveling and she has traveled extensively to different parts of the world. She loves the sophisticated culture of Australia and adores Costa Rica for its significant similarity to Virgin Gorda. She appreciates the relaxed lifestyle and friendly people of Finland as well as the vibrant nature of Spain, its cuisine and its people.

When she is not traveling, she enjoys reading, writing, street fairs, Art Walks, and Afternoon Tea with close friends. She lives in Southern California with her beautiful Rottweiler, Duchess.

www.ingramcontent.com/pod-product-compliance
Lightning Source LLC
Chambersburg PA
CBHW062205080426
42734CB00010B/1798